Can you think of anything more dreadful than that your nature might be resolved into a multiplicity?

Søren Kierkegaard, *Either/Or*

Singleness of Heart

Restoring the Divided Soul

Clifford Williams

WILLIAM B. EERDMANS PUBLISHING COMPANY
GRAND RAPIDS, MICHIGAN

Printed in the United States of America

Library of Congress Cataloging-in-Publication Data

Williams, Clifford, 1943-

Singleness of heart: restoring the divided soul / Clifford Williams.

p.   cm.

Includes bibliographical references.

ISBN 0-8028-0705-4 (pbk.)

1. Spiritual life — Christianity.   I. Title

BV4501.2.W534   1994

248.4 — dc20   94-1518

CIP

Portions of this book are excerpts from "Silence," *Christian Standard,* November 23, 1986, pp. 14-15; "When Mercy Hurts," *Christianity Today,* February 3, 1989, pp. 16-19; "Moral Beauty," *Spirituality Today* 42 (Spring 1990): 4-14; and "Pretending, Self-Justification, and Grace," in *Best Sermons 4,* edited by James W. Cox (San Francisco: HarperCollins, 1991), pp. 258-63. Used with permission.

To those "individuals" who have
unburied their deepest secrets

Contents

Acknowledgments

I want to thank Dave Bertolet, Tom Cavenagh, Colleen Rumley, Larry Shallenberger, and Tom Wetzel for reading the entire book in its formative stages; Kent Anderson, Doug Frank, Alicia Inglis, Ellen Palmer, Neal Plantinga, and Linda Williams for reading parts of it; my classes at Trinity College for listening to some of its contents in the form of weekly meditations; Trinity College for granting me a sabbatical during which I wrote a portion of the book; Oats the vagabond for his restless but searching heart; and all those with whom I have talked about these matters, especially Colleen Rumley and Tom Wetzel, for their encouragement, interest, and illuminating insights. It is from these latter, and from those who have divulged their deepest secrets to me, that I have learned more than any book could teach. To them I dedicate this book.

Preface

The Christian heart is a strange paradox. Though it clings to God tenaciously, it forgets him and flees from him. Though it humbly receives God's forgiveness, it feels that it does not need forgiveness. Sometimes it acts from motives that are alien to its God-commitment; sometimes it pretends, both to others and to itself, to be better than it knows itself to be.

On occasion it is acutely aware of these contradictions and struggles with them. More often, though, it has only a partial awareness or no awareness of them.

This book is an invitation to explore the dividedness that infects the Christian heart. *Singleness of Heart* investigates the ways in which this dividedness is exhibited and probes behind it to concealed and unacknowledged motives.

Accepting this invitation involves risks. It might produce distrust in the genuineness of Christian love or skepticism about whether we can be open to God's grace. It might even lead to unremitting despair about human nature.

However, if the exploration is not made, the reward may never be obtained. Healing requires that the condition needing healing be brought to light. My aim is not to foster distrust, skepticism, or despair. It is to incite single-minded openness to God's grace.

The themes in this book can be found in the works of Dostoyevsky, Pascal, Kierkegaard, Augustine, Tolstoy, Ernest Becker, and the Apostle Paul. These writers were not willing to accept surface appearances as the final truth about human nature. They probed and poked, watched and investigated, not just to discover general truths about humankind but to unearth the truth about themselves. In the work of all of these writers except Tolstoy, grace is presented as the remedy for the trouble within.

I am indebted especially to Augustine's account of his conversion in Book 8 of his *Confessions,* Dostoyevsky's *Crime and Punishment,* Ernest Becker's *The Denial of Death,* Pascal's *Pensées,* and Kierkegaard's *Purity of Heart Is To Will One Thing.*

I remind the reader, as did Kierkegaard, that the writer "has his own life, his own frailties, his own share of doubleness of mind." *Singleness of Heart* is as much confession as it is description of the interior life.

Chapter 1

Introduction: Doubleness and the Pursuit of the Eternal

A secret unrest gnaws at the roots of our being.

Carl Jung, *Psychological Reflections*

Underneath the busyness and drudgery of everyday living, we sense that there is something more to life than the unthinking performance of our daily tasks. We are vaguely aware of a nagging restlessness, and in self-reflective moods we feel empty.

Often we do not know the source of this empty feeling. We are uncomfortable with the way things are but do not know what would satisfy us. Perhaps some new adventure or some kind of excitement. But these too seem hollow from a larger perspective, and we wonder what it would take to quell our uneasiness.

Sometimes, however, we do know what would satisfy us. We may feel lonely and recognize that though we have friends, we want deeper intimacy with them. We may come to realize that we have never exercised compassion and want to find some way of doing so. We may reflect on the inner turmoil we have experienced — anxiety, insecurity, doubt — and want inner serenity. We may have an acute sense of guilt and crave forgiveness, or feel rejected and yearn for acceptance. We may notice that we rarely experience delight or wonder and want to escape the dull torpor we feel trapped in. We may wonder whether our lives have any point, whether there is anything that makes them worthwhile, and want to know that we have lived well. We might become aware that we have never loved without reserve and long to give ourselves away. We may sense that we could love God more and desire to find out how.

These feelings indicate both a dissatisfaction with our current state and a desire for something more. They are expressions of a certain wistfulness — that faraway look in our eye as we sit quietly thinking about life. They spring from our craving for eternity.

This craving moves us to want various emotional and spiritual states. It moves us to want to give and receive love, to want to be free from inner turbulence, and to want to know that God loves us. We desire eternity when we want to be awed by the mystery of God or be drawn out of ourselves with self-forgetful praise. We also desire it when we want to know of the beauty in another's life or when we want to identify with another's pain. The pursuit of eternity is the pursuit of God, of love — of those something more's that we sense are missing from our daily routines.

One manifestation of the craving for eternity is the "homesickness for holiness" that overcame St. Francis of Assisi after his conversion. This intriguing characteristic is described by his biographer as "the longing to give up the thousand things with which the soul vainly creates unrest and perturbation for itself, and to seek the one thing which satisfies."[1]

When we are homesick, we are captive to the desire to return home. We feel ill at ease away from home and cannot rest until our desire to return is satisfied. When we are homesick for eternity, we are unable to be at peace with ourselves until we obtain the something more that we seek.

Two biblical metaphors capture the idea of being homesick for eternity: being hungry and being thirsty. Those who are hungry for what is good will be happy, for they will be filled (Matt. 5:6). The Psalmist longs for God in the same way a thirsty deer longs for a stream of cool water (42:1).

1. Johannes Jorgensen, *St. Francis of Assisi* (New York: Doubleday–Image Books, 1955), p. 61.

When political prisoners or prisoners of war are denied adequate food for extended periods of time, the only thing they can think about is food. They dream of filling meals and luscious desserts. Their one passion is to be able to sit down and eat their favorite foods in the company of family and friends. When those who are in love must part, they ache to be in each other's presence again. Scarcely an hour passes without this ache rising anew a dozen times. A similar longing affects us when we remember the exhilaration of a past love, the reassuring praise of a parent, or the tenderness of a friend's touch. We re-create the experience in our minds, wishing that we could relive it.

It is the same with those who long for eternity. The dominant aim in their lives is to possess eternity. This aim is both a passion and an ache. It is the pursuit of single-minded love without distractions, clutter, or obstructions.

Sometimes we are conscious of our craving for eternity. During such times we have a keen sense of our desire to be loved. We become exhilarated at the prospect of possessing intimacy and inner contentment. These times may not last long. Often, in fact, they are fleeting moments that puncture our reveries and flit in and out of everyday humdrum.

At other times our sense of eternity dims, shoved aside by distractions and evasions. We become absorbed in life's duties, which squeeze out our delight in love. We pursue alien pleasures, which numb our desire to be aware of God more. We deliberately squash the longing for grace we once were conscious of. During these times we are scarcely aware that life contains anything more than what we can hold in our hands.

During still other times we find ourselves pulled in opposite directions, sometimes alternately and sometimes simultaneously. We are open to God's grace, but we continually try to justify ourselves by our good qualities and our successes. We humbly help others without thought of gain for doing so, but secretly think of ourselves as heroes. We derive comfort from realizing that God knows our struggles and troubles, but are afraid of his knowing the secrets we keep hidden even from ourselves. We easily grasp the point of the story of the Pharisee and the tax collector, but immediately point our finger at the Pharisee. We delight in the successes of our acquaintances, but resentment creeps in and undermines that delight. We long for heart-to-heart talks with God, but like John Donne are distracted in our prayers by the noise of a fly.[2]

There are times too when we seek eternity for self-regarding motives. We show compassion to the destitute, hoping to receive their appreciation. We smile warmly at friends to convince them that our spiritual life is without defect. We read Christian books, pray, and help neighbors so that we can feel good about our goodness. In these cases, we act as if we possess eternity when in fact we do not.

Some of the time, then, we possess an untarnished sense of eternity; some of the time we do not possess any sense of it; and some of the time we are divided in one of two ways. In one way we are pulled both toward and away from eternity, and in the other we act from a self-regarding motive that makes it appear, both to others and to ourselves, as if we have eternity.

We should not suppose that we are always conscious of the dividedness in us. Most of the time, in fact, we are probably unconscious of it. We may never suspect that we use our accomplishments and social station to make ourselves feel acceptable to God. We may be only vaguely aware that our feelings about God really come from our fear of parental disapproval. After years of conscientious Christian activity, we may finally wake up to the fact that we have used it simply to impress ourselves with our goodness.

The fact that the dividedness in us is often unconscious means that we are not what we seem to be. In his engaging novel entitled *The Secret Sharer,* Joseph Conrad describes the feeling of a sea captain as he is about to begin a journey on a ship on which he has never

---

2. "I neglect God and his angels for the noise of a fly, for the rattling of a coach, for the whining of a door; I talk on in the same posture of praying, eyes lifted up, knees bowed down, as though I prayed to God; and if God or his angels should ask me when I thought last of God in that prayer, I cannot tell. Sometimes I find that I had forgot what I was about, but when I began to forget it I cannot tell. A memory of yesterday's pleasures, a fear of tomorrow's dangers, a straw under my knee, a noise in mine ear, a light in mine eye, an anything, a nothing, a fancy, a chimera in my brain troubles me in my prayer" (John Donne, "The Divided Mind," Sermon LXXX, in *Seventeenth-Century Prose and Poetry* ed. Robert P. Tristram Coffin and Alexander M. Witherspoon [New York: Harcourt, Brace & World, 1957], p. 115).

before set foot. "What I felt most," says the captain, "was my being a stranger to the ship." Then, in a more pensive mood, he adds, "and if all the truth must be told, I was somewhat of a stranger to myself."

This last remark is so parenthetical that the reader is apt to pass it over without noticing it. It is worth noticing, though. We may think we know ourselves, but often we do not. As the captain observed, we are to some extent strangers to ourselves.

Singleness of Heart searches the secret places of the Christian heart so that we can get beyond the cursory acquaintance we have with ourselves. It uncovers the ways in which dividedness exhibits itself so that we can pursue eternity single-mindedly. The central themes are embodied in the story of the Pharisee and the tax collector told in Luke 18:9-14. Although we are divided, usually without knowing it, we can obtain eternity through mercy — not easy, one-time mercy, but probing, burning mercy. The more we know our dividedness, the more mercy hurts. Yet the more we know our dividedness, the more we can secure — with mercy — the one thing that satisfies.

This book is addressed to those who have experienced the uneasiness that comes when hidden motives poke their way into consciousness. It is directed to those who have felt themselves being pulled in opposite directions, who have become aware of acting for reasons they are reluctant to acknowledge. It is for those who wonder whether their faith is as pure and simple as they once thought it was, and who suspect that continuing to receive mercy may not be so easy as receiving mercy for the first time.

I begin in Chapter 2 with a characterization of singleness and a description of ways we can detect motives that undermine it. I then describe some of these motives in Chapter 3. In Chapter 4 I depict other conditions that impede singleness of heart. In Chapter 5 I focus on a crucial form of dividedness, illusory experiences of grace, in which we mistakenly think we are open to God's grace, and in Chapter 6 I give criteria to test these experiences. I next portray in Chapter 7 what it would be like to live in a community of grace. Before concluding in Chapter 9 with some reflections on singleness and doubleness, I describe in Chapter 8 two other-directed forms of singleness of heart — self-forgetful praise of God and awareness of moral beauty in other people.

Chapter 2

Singleness and Doubleness

We are, I know not how, double in ourselves, so that we believe what we disbelieve, and we cannot rid ourselves of what we condemn.

Montaigne

There are certain things in a man's past, which he does not divulge to everybody but, perhaps, only to his friends. Again there are certain things he will not divulge even to his friends; he will divulge them perhaps only to himself, and that, too, as a secret. But, finally, there are things which he is afraid to divulge even to himself, and every decent man has quite an accumulation of such things in his mind.

Dostoyevsky, *Notes from the Underground*

Before describing motives that undermine singleness of heart, I shall say something about what singleness is and shall describe the self-watching that detecting dividedness requires.

Singleness of Heart

To understand singleness of heart, we must look at the two kinds of dividedness I referred to in the last chapter. In the first kind, ambivalence, we are drawn both toward and away from a given object. In the second kind, illusion, the motive we think we act from differs from the motive we actually act from.

Both the attraction and the aversion in ambivalence are genuine. We are, for example, attracted to God's holiness, but we also shrink from it. We are open to God's grace, but find ourselves justifying our existence by comparing our successes with those of others. In these situations, it is not that we are really fearful of God while just appearing to be attracted to him, or that we are really justifying ourselves while just appearing to be open to grace, as happens in illusion. We are genuinely both attracted and fearful, really both repentant and self-justifying.

Ambivalence is exhibited in a variety of everyday contexts. We may have mixed feelings about our jobs, being both satisfied and discontented with them. We may be attracted to a friend or spouse, perhaps with a great deal of love, yet feel indifference or repulsion as well. At times we may feel enthusiasm and excitement about our projects, yet at other times experience boredom or drudgery. At the very moment we are acting irritably toward a family member, we may be conscious of the patience we told ourselves we would exercise.

Ambivalence is also exhibited in Christian contexts. We know we will be with Christ after we die, yet in unguarded moments we are afraid of death. We delight in God's presence, give him thanks and praise, yet we do not want him to get too close. We may resolve to touch a hurting friend or to ask someone for forgiveness, but say when the time comes to make the telephone call, "It can wait" or "It doesn't matter that much." We may intend to spend more time alone in quiet thinking, but lose interest when other thoughts come rushing along.

Many of these ambivalent feelings spring from stronger and more deep-seated ambivalences toward life's basic realities — love, death, meaning, change, finitude. Toward each of these we feel, underneath the surfaces of our consciousness, both an attraction and an aversion or an acceptance and a defiance. We may have come to terms with the limits of what we can be, but something in us refuses to accept these limits — we crave almost desperately to be big in every way. We may not be content with the course of our lives, wanting creative change and new possibilities, but shrink almost cringingly from newness. We both love and dread love itself. We both seek and run from God. We treat ourselves with generous amounts of attention and solicitude, but also with suspicious uneasiness and sometimes a fair amount of contempt. We want more of life's treasures, yet withdraw almost suicidally when these treasures present themselves.

Ambivalence is not unknown to the biblical writers. One of Jesus' suppliants pleads, "I believe; help my unbelief!" (Mark 9:24). In Romans 7 Paul describes the conflicting inclinations within him: "I do not do what I want, but I do the very thing I hate" (v. 15). And, "So I find it to be a law that when I want to do what is good, evil lies close at hand" (v. 21).

It is important to note that ambivalence is not the same as indifference. Indifference exists when we have no attraction to or aversion from God; we are apathetic and unconcerned. If we are indifferent toward grace, we can take it or leave it without caring one way or the other. When we are ambivalent, however, we care about grace, but we also run from it. We take refuge in grace for forgiveness, but resist it to avoid having to admit guilt. When we are indifferent toward guilt, we have no interest in it, but when we are ambivalent, we have a great deal of interest in it. "I fear and evade my guilt, yet cling to it," writes C. Stephen Evans.[1] Of course, we may have both interest in and indifference toward guilt, in which case we have something akin to attraction and aversion. Indifference by itself, though, is not the same as these opposite pulls.

One intriguing feature of ambivalence is that we can experience both attraction and aversion simultaneously. Although we often want intimacy with a spouse and later fear it, we also on occasion want

---

1. Evans, *Søren Kierkegaard's Christian Psychology* (Grand Rapids, Mich.: Zondervan Publishing Co., 1990), p. 64.

it and fear it at the same time. In struggling to accept our finitude, we sometimes accept it and defy it alternately, but other times we do both concurrently. It is the same with grace and self-justification, selflessness and selfishness, creative love and self-enclosing retreat. We go both ways, not just one after the other, but at once.

The presence of these oppositions is unsettling because it creates doubts about who we really are and what we really want. Do we really love our parents or do we hate them? Have we really given a gift without expectation of return, or have we given it to get something back? Are we really self-centered persons parading as good and loving Christians?

The answer to these questions is that if in these instances we are genuinely ambivalent, then we are both selfless and self-centered, accepting and judgmental. We are not just one side of the ambivalent dyad, though we want to think so. We are both. We really are open to grace, even though we also really try to justify our existence with successful performance. We really do praise God disinterestedly, though we also really expect him to make us important. These oppositions cannot be explained away as our being one thing while appearing to be something else.

The situation is different with illusion. In it our real motives for acting are different from the motives we think we act from. If we engage in volunteer activities, thinking that we do so in order to help needy people, but really do so in order to be noticed by those whose esteem we value, we are in a state of illusion. We are also in a state of illusion if our submerged motive for greeting acquaintances with large and friendly smiles is to be known as outgoing, or if we join a prayer group merely to demonstrate to others that our Christianity is not deficient. The dividedness in these cases consists of a public posture that is at variance with an inner reality. It also consists of a private posture that is at variance with an inner reality. We seem to others and to ourselves to be one thing when in reality we are something else.

Consider openness to grace again. When we are ambivalent, we are genuinely open to grace but struggle with the impulse to justify ourselves by displays of success. When we act under illusion, we act to satisfy this impulse without being open to grace. We think we are open to grace, but the inner reality belies this thought. Similarly, when we are ambivalent about love, we sincerely love selflessly, though lurking beside, but not behind, our selflessness are self-directed motives. When we act under illusion, however, we appear to be loving selflessly, but behind this appearance and not just beside it are motives of gain. We merely look as if we love. In actuality we do not.

As we shall see in the next chapter, the motives that incite illusion, like the drives from which ambivalence springs, are deep-seated and tenacious. Compensating for our sense of unworth lies behind our associating with certain people. The drive to make ourselves bigger and more important makes us say things we know our listeners will be impressed with. The need to justify our existence causes us to do things other people will notice and admire.

We are now in a position to describe singleness of heart. We possess singleness when we are not pulled in opposite directions and when we act without wanting something further for ourselves. Our inner drives do not conflict; they are aimed in one direction. The motives we appear to have are the ones we really have. Our inner focus is unified and our public posture corresponds with it. We are not, in short, divided in either of the two ways I have described.

Consider two everyday examples: listening and playing. During most one-on-one listening, we think mainly of how our concerns relate to what the other person is telling us or of what astute response we can make. Our aim, unconscious though it may be, is to preserve a sense of worth for ourselves, to make sure that we get our share of attention. When, however, we become absorbed in what someone is saying without having these half-conscious aims, we acquire singleness. This can happen when we identify with the hurts and pains of a friend who is unburdening herself. For a moment we are present to her without needing to get something out of the conversation for ourselves.

Our playing too is infected with the need to prove that we are as good as other players. To lose is to be a failure. Though we tell ourselves that playing is just a game, inside we really feel that the stakes are high. Young children, however, appear to play differently.

At times they seem to be so completely absorbed in their play that they forget themselves and focus entirely on what they are doing. They do not appear to be thinking about who they want to impress or how good they are at rearranging kitchen pots. For fleeting moments we adults may possess the same kind of singleness. We lose ourselves in a game, playing solely for the sake of playing, not caring if we win or lose.

Singleness of heart has the same childlike unconcern. Those who give without expecting some return have this unconcern, as do those who love for the sake of loving. When we experience God's forgiveness without feeling that we must do something to earn it, or when we sense God's presence without fearing that he will invade us, we are free from the cares that produce division in us. Our hearts are not cluttered with conflicting compulsions or ego-enhancing impulses.

Having this childlike unconcern does not mean we will be superficial. Singleness of heart is not the same as lacking in depth or intensity, nor does it consist of just one emotion. The person possessing singleness may indeed feel deeply and intensely in many ways. She may feel the pain of a dying friend; she may be aware of the rejection felt by minorities and those who are poor, unemployed, or old; she may identify with others' loneliness, despair, and disappointment. She may delight in the accomplishments and happiness of friends; she herself may have moments of deep contentment or spontaneous merriment; she may notice the changing moods of acquaintances and be alert for needed encouragement.

In searching for singleness of heart, we are searching for depth — the depth of earnest love, wholehearted giving, unfeigned tenderness, and heartfelt admiration. We are also searching for transparency in this depth. Extraneous cravings and distracting desires are not visible in it, nor are hidden motives and ambivalent drives. This depth has the clearness of an unmuddied sea. "No storm may perturb it; no sudden gust of wind may stir its surface, no drowsy fog may sprawl out over it; no doubtful movement may stir within it; no swift-moving cloud may darken it: rather it must lie calm, transparent to its depth."[2]

2. Søren Kierkegaard, *Purity of Heart Is to Will One Thing*, trans. Douglas V. Steere (New York: Harper, 1956), p. 176.

11

Why Pursue Singleness?

It is useful to ask at this point, "Why pursue singleness?" Why must compassionate action be free from ambivalence and illusion? If the action itself makes a difference in other people's lives, why does it matter what our motives are?

There are several responses to these questions. One is that we do not want to be divided. One of the basic drives of human nature is to possess singleness. The discovery that we have engaged in loving behavior to get something for ourselves makes us uneasy, as does the thought that we might be different from what we think we are. We want to be free from motives that pull us in opposite ways; we do not like being victims of illusion.

This drive for singleness is, to be sure, blunted by motives that undermine it. And because these motives attract us, there is a sense in which dividedness attracts us. We like being admired by other Christians for our virtuous actions even though we want to be virtuous for its own sake. We do not want to dispel our illusions because we prefer to think that our love has no self-interested motives. Nevertheless, something in us is discontent with the ambivalence and illusion that charm us so. Sometimes we are conscious of this discontent, and sometimes we are barely aware of it. In either case, the discontent points to the presence of an underlying desire for singleness.

A second reason for pursuing singleness is that other people do not want to be recipients of our self-justifying motives, just as we do not want to be recipients of their self-justifying motives. They do not want us to love them so that we can be admired by those who notice what we do. Nor do we want others to love us so that they can be admired. They would feel demeaned if they knew we used them to obtain admiration, and we would feel degraded if we knew they used us to obtain admiration. With singleness of heart, however, loving is engaged in for its own sake. This is the kind of love other people desire, and it is the kind of love we crave as well.

The same is true of our love for God. God wants our love for him to be free from self-interested motives. He does not want us to love him for what we get from doing so — the feeling of superiority over those who do not love him, for example, or the love he will

12

give us in return. If we were to love God for these reasons, we would be manipulating him in the same way we would be manipulating people if we loved them for self-interested motives. God, we may safely say, does not want to be manipulated any more than we do.

Underlying these reasons for pursuing singleness of heart is the perception of its goodness. We want singleness, not just because its presence dispels the discomfort that ambivalence and illusion bring, but because we see that it is good to possess. It is in fact a very great good, and our recognition that this is so propels us toward it. Our attraction to it is somewhat like the attraction we have to intricately designed works of art or to natural panoramas that evoke breathtaking awe. We gaze at them, not because of what they do for us, but because of their beauty. In singleness of heart, too, we see a thing of great beauty.

We also see that single-minded motives are good because of what they can do for those to whom they are directed. Words of affirmation, for example, can produce in their recipients a sense of worth that does not depend on satisfactory performance. This sense of worth can in turn be instrumental in the emotional healing of the person to whom the words are directed. Part of what makes this healing possible is the perception of the single-minded attitude in the affirmer, an attitude that conceives of the affirmed person as an individual having intrinsic value, not as an object to be used. We perceive, then, that having a single-minded attitude is good in the same way that giving is good — both in itself and for the effect it can have on the receiver.

From these observations about pursuing singleness, however, we must not infer that we should refrain from acting compassionately unless we know we have single-minded motives. It is better to act compassionately knowing that, try as we may to prevent it, we will have self-regarding motives, than it is not to act compassionately at all. My reason for saying this is that an exploration of our secrets is likely to lead to a fair amount of skepticism about whether we can ever be entirely free of self-regarding motives. And this skepticism may make us reluctant to act at all. We may feel that doing so without pure motives has no value. As the authors of *Compassion* point out, however, "We can never claim pure motives, and it is better to act with and for those who suffer than to wait until we have our own needs completely under control."[3] If we felt obliged to wait until we had singleness of heart in order to act compassionately, we would never act compassionately, just as we would never get married if we felt we had to be perfectly mature in order to do so.

In what follows I assume that we want singleness, that we believe it to be a shining jewel that we will go to great lengths to obtain, and that we want to uncover our dividedness (but also that we are afraid to uncover it). I do not assume that actions performed without singleness have no value whatever.

Detecting Dividedness

Augustine gives an absorbing account of the conflict he experienced as he neared the moment of his conversion. He was convinced that it was better to give himself to God's love than to give in to his own desires. But, he writes, "although the one way appealed to me and was gaining mastery, the other still afforded me pleasure and kept me victim." He prayed, "Give me chastity and continence, but not yet!" He was afraid that God would hear his prayer and heal him of his addiction to lust sooner than he wanted. The intensity of his inner strife "laid waste" his soul, and the tumult within became a "raging combat" that he engaged in against himself.[4]

Although the struggle Augustine experienced before his conversion is like the ambivalence Christians experience after their conversions, it differs in two respects. First, because Augustine had not yet yielded to God's transforming mercy, he merely wanted it, whereas Christians actually have it. Augustine possessed the old but wanted the new, whereas Christians who experience ambivalence possess the new but still are pulled toward the old.

3. Donald P. McNeill, Douglas A. Morrison, and Henri J. M. Nouwen, *Compassion: A Reflection on the Christian Life* (New York: Doubleday–Image Books, 1983), p. 122.

4. Augustine, *Confessions,* trans. John K. Ryan (New York: Doubleday–Image Books, 1960), Book 8, Chapters 5, 7, 8, pp. 189, 194, 195.

Second, much of our dividedness is not as explicit as was Augustine's. We sometimes cherish superiority or bask in the warm glow of self-admiration without noticing that we do. Often we are unaware of the lure of self-justification or of our distracting activities. Or we feel the lure vaguely and are half-conscious of our distractions. Numbness characterizes us as much as, perhaps more than, does raging combat.

Discovering dividedness, therefore, is not always a simple matter. It is in fact rarely a simple matter. There is so much in us that is hidden and so much that we resist knowing that it may take years of effort to bring some motives to full awareness. In the following sections I shall describe several methods that can be used to do this. These methods are not special techniques that only trained psychologists can use; they are part of what it means for anyone to be a self-watcher.

Inspecting Our Inner Newsreels

One of the prominent though scarcely acknowledged facts about our minds is that they are constantly active in between the times when we talk and act. During these times, a continuous and often disconnected series of thoughts, feelings, and images occupies our minds. We run over the conversation we just had, glowing with good feeling because someone has noticed something distinctive about us. We remember last night's visit with a friend and think of tomorrow's long-awaited get-together with another friend. The image of someone with whom we have had some difficulty pops into consciousness, and for an instant a negative feeling comes, but it leaves just as quickly when the question of how we are going to finish a pressing task arises.

Sometimes these fleeting thoughts arise while we are doing something, such as making supper, driving a car, or talking with someone. They come too during the minutes just before we fall asleep and again just before we get out of bed in the morning. We cannot make our minds stop for long. New thoughts come rushing along whenever we try.

Ernest Becker calls these series of thoughts, feelings, and images "inner newsreels."[5] Usually we are relatively unaware of what goes on in them, or even that they exist. If we could stop their rapid rush and inspect them, we would come to know what we really love and what really bothers us. We would find the motives underlying our life's projects and the reasons for the things we say.

Imagine, for example, that the image of a friend comes to mind. A feeling of warm approval accompanies the image, especially when the image is conjoined with the thought of the person watching us doing something. We must, then, want the approval of this friend. What we do becomes satisfying partly because we imagine ourselves being watched. Now imagine that we picture ourselves being congratulated for an accomplishment or being admired for something we have made or simply being liked. Here too there is a feeling of warm satisfaction accompanying the images. What we want, these images reveal, is to be admired and liked. What we feel, perhaps unconsciously, is that we are not admired and liked.

Inspecting our inner newsreels in Christian contexts can be somewhat unsettling. Suppose some Sunday morning, before we have left for church, the thought occurs to us that it would be nice to stay home and write letters. Immediately there flashes to mind the image of acquaintances at church. We are telling them why we stayed home and feeling somewhat apprehensive about doing so. The image leaves as quickly as it comes; we do not reflect on it or mull it over. Nor do we stay home and write letters. At church we say hello to those acquaintances with a smile, feeling half-consciously a sense of relief that we did not have to explain our absence to them. This segment of our inner newsreels may be telling us that our reason for being at church is the fear of real or imagined disapproval. It may also be telling us that this fear is masquerading as Christian commitment.

5. Becker, *The Birth and Death of Meaning,* 2d ed. (New York: Macmillan–The Free Press, 1972), pp. 68-69.

Observing Actions

If we want to know what values people adhere to, we look at what they do — the way they spend their spare time, the books they read, the clothes they wear, the friends they talk to, the entertainment they engage in, the things they like to talk about, the places they visit. If we want to know what people are feeling, we look at their actions and facial expressions — the fleeting look of anxiety on their faces when they think no one is looking, the worried tone of voice, the fidgety hands, the enthusiastic response to a gift received, the initiative taken to make contacts with friends. If there is a conflict between their behavior and what they say they feel, we tend to trust what their behavior reveals to us. We would, for example, believe that a friend is still hurt by a cutting remark in spite of protestations to the contrary if we noticed an angry look on her face.

The principle on which our observations are based is that there is a connection between people's actions and what they think, value, and feel. This principle is embodied in Jesus' statement, "You will know them by their fruits" (Matt. 7:16). What he meant was that we can tell what people are like by looking at how they act. Our first reaction to this principle is that it is indeed a way to discover what other people are like. It is unnerving, however, to think that the principle applies to us as well, that others can use it to find out what we are like, and, further, that we can use it to find out what we are like.

When we notice people spending a great deal of time trying to be successful at their careers, we infer that the driving force of their lives is the need for esteem and importance. When we notice ourselves making strenuous efforts to achieve success, we can justly make the same inference. Saying witty and clever things to acquaintances often belies a desire for admiration, and if we catch ourselves saying such things, it is probably because we have that desire. If we engage in mind-numbing activities, we may be fleeing from the knowledge of uncomfortable truths about ourselves. If we feel our faces becoming tight, we know that we have become angry.

The point here is that we can discover what we are feeling and thinking without directly inspecting our inner states. We know the kinds of attitudes that normally accompany actions and facial expressions. So by observing our own actions, we can uncover our attitudes.

Imagining

We can also get through to our hidden attitudes by using our imagination in creative ways. We can imagine being other people who are looking at us and ask how they see us. What would they think about what we just said? What inferences would they make about our motives based on their observations of our actions? We can imagine having the feelings that others have, partly to learn to distinguish different kinds of feelings and partly to discover our own. We can imagine ourselves talking with others, revealing things about ourselves that we would be afraid to reveal in an actual conversation. We can imagine talking with God, who searchingly but lovingly opens our hearts. We can imagine for a day that we are facing the imminent prospect of death and notice what our reactions are.

What lies behind these methods of detecting dividedness is the desire to look and listen. This desire does not accept appearances; it wants to search, and it asks questions. The opposite attitude is indifference. This attitude accepts appearances and does not ask questions. It is content not to listen.

Perhaps someone will ask, "Why must we look inside ourselves so extensively? Why can't we simply love spontaneously? Doesn't genuine love require us to focus our attention on other people? Wouldn't the pursuit of hidden motives breed self-centeredness and a morbid fascination with fallen human nature? And doesn't Christ's redemption free us from these?"

The answer is that we may think we are loving selflessly when in fact we are moved by the hope of some return. We may believe we are moving in a Godward direction even though we are driven by the desire to be better than others. To find out whether we are what we appear to be, we have to poke around behind the appearances.

Moreover, if we are not aware of our unconscious motives, they will control us. We will not be able genuinely to focus our attention on other people if we are continually admiring ourselves. We will not be able to give ourselves away if our chief motivation is to justify our own existence, or to love if we want merely to obtain esteem.

The truth about human nature is that it possesses a complex and often hidden inner life. Children may be able to love spontaneously, but we adults must exert great effort to recapture the uncontaminated spontaneity of childhood. We have acquired baggage that must be cast off. We have learned how to earn praise, how to appear good, and how to repress guilt and failure. We have become adept at pleasing others in order to justify ourselves and at appearing to love in order to obtain reward.

To root out these hidden drives, we must become aware of them. This requires a sometimes painful self-watching, demanding on occasion excruciating effort. Singleness of heart cannot be acquired by making a one-time resolve. It must be earned "slowly and honestly," as Kierkegaard observed in *Purity of Heart*.[6]

Christ's redemption does indeed free us from our hidden drives — not instantaneously, but progressively, for these drives remain with us throughout our lives. Christ's acceptance increasingly roots out our craving for honor and enables us, bit by bit, to let go of our attachment to self-justification. This rooting out and letting go are at the core of Christian living. They are the crux of our lifetime search for singleness of heart.

The self-watching required for this search does not guarantee singleness of heart. There are in fact definite dangers in self-watching. We can use it to wallow in our own misery, to confirm feelings of failure, and to perpetuate negative feelings about ourselves. We can proudly vindicate our sinfulness with it, or we can use it to abuse ourselves by intensifying guilt feelings that reinforce an already unhealthy sense of being bad. It can undermine self-acceptance.

Self-watching can also become incapacitating by making us unduly depressed or inordinately preoccupied with ourselves. It can produce too much self-consciousness and bring about more inner

6. Kierkegaard, *Purity of Heart Is to Will One Thing*, p. 117.

turbulence. It can become an addiction that thwarts the exercise of compassion. If it results in irremediable doubt about whether we can escape self-justification, it will lead to despair. We may lose the awareness that God loves us.

To avoid these dangers and to prevent self-examination from becoming the goal of Christian living instead of a means only, we must consciously remind ourselves of what we are after. We want to be freed from the habits of comparing and seeking reward, from the impulses to admire and justify ourselves. We want to love with a childlike instinctiveness — automatically and unselfconsciously. We want to be healed of the wounds caused by fear of disapproval and a sense of unworth. We want to be awakened to new realities and enlarge our constricted horizons. We want to know that we really are open to grace.

Augustine's agonizing self-observation revealed to him "two wills, the one old, the other new, the first carnal, and the second spiritual." Although he desperately wanted to resolve the conflict between these two wills, he also did not want to know about it, so he refused to look at it and put what he had already glimpsed out of his memory. When he gazed inward again, he pretended not to see what was there. He found, however, that he could not continue to resist: "the day had come when I stood stripped naked before myself."

Yet Augustine could not endure this intense self-gazing, either, for it was a torment, "bringing with it a mighty downpour of tears." He opened the New Testament and, upon reading the chapter on which his eyes first fell, found the peace for which he longed: "as if before a peaceful light streaming into my heart, all the dark shadows of doubt fled away." The tortuous division dissipated: "Now was my mind free from the gnawing cares of favor-seeking, of striving for gain, of wallowing in the mire, and of scratching lust's itchy sore." He notes, however, that the temptation to seek reward was still present, for he was afraid that public knowledge of his conversion would make people think that he "wanted to look like a big man." To avoid outward show, he at first told only his mother and a close friend, and only later told others.[7]

7. Augustine, *Confessions,* Book 8, Chapters 5, 7, 12, pp. 189, 194, 201, 202; and Book 9, Chapters 1 and 2, pp. 205-6, 207.

Chapter 3

Motives Undermining
Singleness of Heart

*When Christ says (Matthew 10:17), "Beware of men," I wonder
if this is not also meant: Beware of men, lest by men — that
is, by everlasting comparison with other men, by customs and
externals — you let yourself be tricked out of the highest good.
For the chicaneries of a betrayer are not very dangerous, since
one is the more readily alerted to them; but this, to have the
highest good in a sort of indifferent fellowship, in the indolence
of habit, yes, in the indolence of a habit which even sets up
the generation in place of the individual, making the generation
the recipient and the individual a sharer automatically on the
strength of this — this is a terrible thing.*

Søren Kierkegaard, *Works of Love*

Who can untie this most twisted and intricate mass of knots?

Augustine, *Confessions*

In this chapter I shall describe motives that undermine singleness
of heart. These motives produce ambivalence and illusion with
respect to Christian virtues such as compassion and also with respect
to what many regard as the central Christian attitude — that of being

21

open to God's grace. In addition, these motives undercut the vibrancy of a community of grace, a community in which people give grace to one another without wanting anything in return.

The Desire for Reward

We act for the sake of reward when we act in order to obtain something from what we do. We work in order to be paid, cook in order to eat, and drive in order to go places. In these cases there is clearly nothing unacceptable in acting to obtain rewards. We do not have ulterior motives, and we are not disguising our true aims in acting as we do. Cooking is supposed to be done in order to eat.

The situation would be different if we were to act virtuously for some end other than being virtuous. If we were to act compassionately in order to evoke admiration from those who observe us, we would be trying to get something from an activity that should be done for its own sake. In the same way, we would be using a friend for our own purposes if our friendship were aimed at raising our social status. The friendship would not be engaged in for itself.

In these cases we would be using people merely as means for our own ends, or, as Irvin Yalom puts it, as equipment.[1] Other people would be nothing more than tools for us to use to get something for ourselves. This would be true even if we used them to get something good, such as gratitude or love. These responses may, to be sure, be legitimate consequences of compassion and friendship, but if receiving them is our only motive for being compassionate or friendly, we would still be using others simply as equipment.

The distinction between using people and not using them can be illustrated as follows. Imagine that we become friends with someone whom we subsequently find out is unemployed and unable to buy enough food for herself and her aging mother. We would not feel that she was using us simply to obtain aid if she never com-

---

1. "Where one's primary motive in engaging others is to ward off loneliness, then one has transformed the other into equipment" (Irvin D. Yalom, *Existential Psychotherapy* [New York: Basic Books, 1980], pp. 376-77).

plained about her plight, never in fact mentioned it, and was genuinely interested in us. But we would feel used if she informed us of her situation in a complaining tone of voice and seemed to want nothing more from us than money. Though we would gladly give aid in the first case, we would be reluctant to do so in the second.

The same distinction exists with respect to deeply embedded psychological needs. If we were taking part in a conversation in which there was genuine give-and-take between us and another person, we would not feel that we were being used merely to fulfill our partner's need to express herself. But we would feel used if we felt that the person to whom we were talking simply wanted to satisfy her need for self-expression. We would want to continue the first conversation but would want to withdraw from the second. We would also want to withdraw if we felt that someone were secretly acting in certain ways only to get our love or to alleviate loneliness. Though we recognize the legitimacy of these needs, we would not want to be manipulated into satisfying them. And though we would freely meet them if asked straightforwardly to do so, we would resent being maneuvered into doing so.

It is acutely unsettling to realize that we use others in the very ways in which we resent their using us. We feel that we need a certain level of self-importance, so we attach ourselves to those from whom we can get it. We want to be admired, so we say things that others will esteem. When we become desperate for attention, we act in ways that will make people notice us. These motives press us relentlessly to use others for our own purposes. This is true even when what we want is good. Instead of asking, we adroitly guide circumstances to get what we want.

Our desire for reward operates in subtle ways. The look of appreciation on the face of a homeless person to whom we have handed a bowl of soup, a thank-you note from someone to whom we have given a gift, words of affirmation, a smile, the mere mention of our name — all can act as self-enhancing inducements to act virtuously. So can the sense of power we obtain from giving to one who is less well off than we, and the gratification we get when we notice people looking at us.

The desire for reward is exhibited not only in our desire for actual admiration but in our desire for imagined admiration as well. We do not need to be seen by others to obtain reward from them. We can secretly imagine them watching us and smiling with warm approval. They are internal observers who reward us for our virtue even though they do not know about it. We carry these internal observers with us and notice them looking at us when the attraction of compassion for its own sake is not enough. We also notice them observing our thoughts, our attitudes, and even our prayers. We may go to our secret rooms and close the door to pray, but these ubiquitous spectators come too.

When the desire for reward motivates us, what we really want is to get others' approval instead of to love and be virtuous. We sense, half-consciously, that we can get this approval by appearing to love and appearing to be virtuous.

A woman who loves a wealthy man solely because of his wealth is in the same position. She has replaced genuine love with the assurance and esteem of wealth. Her love, though it appears real, is a pseudo-love because what she really wants is something else. The protagonist in Camus's *A Happy Death* illustrates this: "He saw that what had attached him to Martha was vanity[,] not love. . . . What he had loved in Martha were those evenings when they would walk into the movie theater and men's eyes turned towards her, that moment when he offered her to the world. What he had loved in her was his power and his ambition to live."[2]

The same is true for loving in order to be loved. If all that we want from loving is to obtain love in return, we do not in reality want to love. Our love is merely a means to satisfy cravings to be loved. Love must be given without desire for return, or it is not love at all.

On the other hand, the woman who loves a wealthy man simply because of who he is has eyes just for him and not for his wealth. Her love has its own reward: an inner contentment that does not need the assurance and esteem of wealth. Those with singleness of heart are moved only by love and not by what they obtain from

2. Camus, *A Happy Death* (New York: Alfred A. Knopf, 1972), pp. 81-82.

loving. Their reward is quiet joy and release from the restlessness of discordant drives.

The difference between reward as a self-enhancing motive and the reward that is intrinsic to love is captured in Father Zossima's exhortation in Dostoyevsky's *The Brothers Karamazov:* "Never seek reward, for your reward on earth is great as it is: your spiritual joy which only the righteous feel."[3] The reward that is intrinsic to love is happiness in the loving itself, not a reason for the sake of which we love.

It is important to notice that loving without thought of reward does not mean that we disdain everything we receive from loving. Those who love single-mindedly will be noticed, and people will respond in various ways.[4] Some of these responses we should be suspicious of, such as public acclaim or continual attention. Other responses we may gladly accept, such as mutual sharing with friends or assuagement of loneliness. Loving others without thought of return does not preclude needing and seeking to be loved. What it precludes is loving in order to be loved. Though we will receive love when we give love, we cannot think of what we get as a reward without turning what we give into pseudo-love.

It is easy for others to think that we love for its own sake and not for what we get from loving. The woman who loves a wealthy man acts in all the ways that love requires: she pays him attention, overlooks his faults, affirms him, and gives him encouragement. These practices may disguise her attachment to his wealth. So, too, the caring and loving of devout Christians may mask their attraction to the approval they seek from other Christians.

It is also easy for *us* not to know that we act for the sake of reward. We might think we act solely out of love because we imagine that our motives are as pure as our actions are. Or we might hide our rewards from ourselves because we do not want to know we act for their sake.

3. Dostoyevsky, *The Brothers Karamazov,* trans. David Magarshack (New York: Penguin Books, 1958), p. 379.

4. "Those who love a pure heart and are gracious in speech will have the king as a friend" (Prov. 22:11).

We can discover our real motives if we imagine ourselves disclosing them to God. If we know that we cannot hide our secrets from someone who already knows them, our ability to hide them from ourselves is undercut.[5] By opening ourselves to God's knowledge, we will discover whether we want esteem for our loving. We will find out how much of our Christian posture is the product of a desire to obtain others' approval.

The Fear of Disapproval

Acting for the sake of reward is the same as acting to avoid being the recipient of reward's opposite.[6] If we conform to a group's expectations in order to gain a sense of worth, we are trying to ward off a sense of unworth. And if we act virtuously in order to get others' approval, we are aiming at forestalling their disapproval. I want now to focus on the disapproval we so desperately avoid.

Our fear of disapproval is intense. Criticism, rejection, and belittlement cut wounds in us that rarely heal. A disparaging tone of voice and a slighting facial expression injure us. Being shunned or thought inferior makes us feel worthless, and receiving low grades in school or criticism from superiors at work creates feelings of failure. The mere attitude "You're different," which we sometimes sense in others, can cause us to cringe.

The fear of other people's disapproval hovers in the background of nearly all that we do. We work hard at our jobs so we will not receive disdain for inadequate performance. We wear stylish clothes, drive new cars, and keep our lawns neatly trimmed to avoid receiving

---

5. "Much that you are able to keep hidden in darkness, you first get to know by your opening it to the knowledge of the all-knowing One" (Søren Kierkegaard, *Purity of Heart Is to Will One Thing*, trans. Douglas V. Steere [New York: Harper, 1956], p. 51).

6. "The other aspect of the reward-centered man is willing the good only out of fear of punishment. For in essence, this is the same as to will the Good for the sake of the reward, to the extent that avoiding an evil is an advantage of the same sort as that of attaining a benefit" (Kierkegaard, *Purity of Heart Is to Will One Thing*, p. 79).

contemptuous looks. We live in certain neighborhoods, join certain organizations, and adopt certain viewpoints to prevent others' scorn.

Both the intensity and the pervasiveness of our fear of disapproval should make us ask whether we act in religious ways for the same reason. Do we arrive early at the Sunday-morning church service, sing with feeling, and smile profusely afterwards so we will not be thought spiritually inferior? Do we participate in our church's activities and adopt its beliefs to forestall disapproval? Do we profess to be loving; do we profess even to love God, to have repented and received Christ into our hearts, for fear of this disapproval?

The story of the Pharisee and the tax collector invites us to ask these uncomfortable questions. The Pharisee carefully acted in religiously approved ways. He did not dare cheat, lie, or forego tithing for fear of the fingerpointing of his peers if they were to discover that he had done these things. Though he may have thought that what he did was motivated by love for God, it was not.

If the Pharisee could have peered inward (we can scarcely imagine him doing so), he might have discovered that his display of intelligence, strength, and self-control resulted from his vaguely felt awareness of other people's scrutiny. He might have noticed that his level of spiritual energy increased when he knew that he was being watched. Perhaps he would have uncovered the warm satisfaction he felt when he saw how impressed his co-religionists were with his maintenance of orthodoxy.

The Pharisee epitomizes the difference between public appearance and inner reality. The public appearance is admirable — the Pharisee's actions are, after all, to be emulated. The inner reality, however, does not fit with these virtues.

The discovery of this inner reality is the discovery of what really motivates us. If we constantly fear others' judgments, then that is for us the most important thing of all. It controls us in spite of our belief that love of what is good motivates us. The same is true of our profession of faith. If its origin is fear of what our parents, minister, church, or friends would think if we gave it up, then it is no faith at all. Devotion to God does not move us, but the thought of our appearance before others does.

Fear of disapproval operates especially intensely in Christian contexts, as Kierkegaard noted in his *Attack upon "Christendom."* He writes, "Where all are Christians, the situation is this: to call oneself a Christian is the means whereby one secures oneself against all sorts of inconveniences and discomforts . . . and orthodoxy flourishes in the land, no heresy, no schism, orthodoxy everywhere, the orthodoxy which consists in playing the game of Christianity."[7]

Kierkegaard's "attack" was directed at a nineteenth-century state church in Denmark, where everyone was born a Christian, officially proclaimed so at one's baptism as an infant. Kierkegaard's revealing insight in this passage is that being in a Christian group — a church, Bible study, prayer group, or Christian college — tends to produce imitation Christianity. We Christians have an especially strong fear of other Christians' disapproval, and this incites us to play Christianity as a game.

Playing Christianity as a game is going through the motions without the inner reality. It is pretending to be a Christian instead of being one for real, performing as we think others think Christians should perform, trying to convince them that we are worth something. We act in ways we know our Christian group approves of, use the right words to describe our faith, and avoid behavior we know brings disapproval. In a sense, our acts and words, even our feelings, are not our own. Our faith is someone else's. We are impersonators.

We are bright and cheerful to make others think we are victorious Christians. We keep unacceptable emotions locked up, but appropriately display other emotions to prevent people from thinking that something is wrong with us. We refrain from confessing our struggles so we will not appear to be weak. At the same time, when we do confess our difficulties, we sense that we are admired for our honesty. Here we give up one game to play another.

We play the game of Christianity not only for other people but for God as well. The idea of performing for God is hinted at in John Cheever's story entitled "The Lowboy": "Some people make less of an adventure than a performance of their passions. They do not seem

7. Kierkegaard, *Attack upon "Christendom,"* trans. Walter Lowrie (Princeton: Princeton University Press, 1968), pp. 27-28.

to fall in love and make friends but to cast, with men, women, children, and dogs, some stirring drama. . . . Watching my brother, I feel that he has marshalled a second-rate cast and that he is performing, perhaps for eternity, the role of a spoiled child."[8] When we perform for eternity, we act, with God as our audience, the role of what we conceive a good Christian to be.

Because playing at Christianity springs from fear of disapproval, part of us secretly wants to play. Yet another part of us does not want to do so. We do not want to have a simulated Christianity or a simulated life because we have a deep desire for a unified consciousness. So we are caught in a dilemma: on the one hand, we want to pretend because doing so salves a desperate fear, but on the other hand, we want to be rid of pretending.

The way out of this dilemma is to adopt the tax collector's perspective. Adopting the tax collector's perspective means obtaining worth from God's grace, not from other Christians' approval. It means being free from the tyranny of maintaining appearances. Embracing the tax collector's attitude releases us to be ourselves instead of what we conceive others want us to be, and frees us to have our own faith instead of someone else's. It stirs us to quit playing Christianity as a game.

When we adopt the tax collector's attitude, we set aside our impulse to be admired by other Christians for our Christianity. We give up our desire for people to like us for living up to accepted standards. The fear of disapproval no longer motivates us. We can be part of a Christian group without constantly worrying about whether we are good enough for others in the group.

Adopting the tax collector's attitude does not mean that we will demean ourselves or grovel in the thought that we are worms which are loathsome even to touch. We will, to be sure, know what we are like inside, unlike the Pharisee. But we will not savor that knowledge. We will move beyond it, as the tax collector did, and accept ourselves in the same way God accepts us.

8. Cheever, "The Lowboy," in *Christian Short Stories,* ed. Mark Booth (New York: Crossroad Publishing Co., 1984), p. 192.

The Drive for Self-justification

One of our rock-bottom needs is to feel that our existence has worth. We want to know that we are acceptable and that our existence matters. This need for a sense of worth turns sour, though, when we use illegitimate means, such as wealth or social status, to satisfy it. It also turns sour when our motive for loving or acting compassionately is to prove our worth. In both of these cases, we are using others as tools to justify our own existence.

The need to feel that our existence has worth exhibits itself from the earliest days of infancy, when the warmth of our mother's body gives us the feeling of being loved, to the latest days of old age, when we wonder whether our lives have been worthwhile. In between, it drives us to work at certain kinds of jobs, seek friends, join groups, get married, and create a place for ourselves in a social network.

The sense of worth is not just feeling good about ourselves, though that is part of it. The sense of worth is the sense of mattering; it is the feeling of having significance and value. When we do something that we believe has made a difference to someone, we feel that we ourselves have worth. When someone compliments us for an accomplishment or for our clothes, we feel that our existence has been validated. Working faithfully at a job also gives us this sense of validation, as does a pay raise. So does having friends with whom we share our inner emotional life.

Simply satisfying the need for a sense of worth is not objectionable. What is objectionable is satisfying that need in distorted and exaggerated ways. We find worth in distorted ways when we put others down with critical remarks, exercise power over them, or build a sense of independence that distances us from them. We exaggerate when we are not content simply with having friends but want to have important friends, or when we are not satisfied with aiding someone in distress but want to be the best aider or the hero who has rescued a hopeless situation from catastrophe. The extreme form of exaggeration is to think of oneself as a world hero, as one who is superior to everyone else.

Distortion and exaggeration spring from a keen sense of unworth.

We possess a sense of unworth when we feel that we are failures or that we are not as good as someone else at doing something. Being criticized can cause it, and so can the lack of compliments or simply not being noticed. Parental expectations that we never seem able to fulfill can bring about a strong sense of unworth. The same is true when we do not meet performance standards of an employer, a teacher, or a coach. When someone wins an award that we ourselves wanted or becomes more well-known and well-liked than we are, we may instinctively feel devalued. In more extreme cases, we may feel that our lives make no difference to anyone, that nothing we do counts for anything, and that it does not matter whether we live or die.

We can discover the extent to which the sense of unworth influences us by noticing the contents of our inner newsreels. Almost all of them contain images that involve, directly or indirectly, our need for a sense of worth. We remember a conversation we had with a friend or the point we made in a group discussion, and we smile to ourselves because of what we said. The face of a person of the opposite sex flashes to mind along with the feeling of being admired. We imagine ourselves greeting newcomers at church and contributing generously to charitable organizations, and we warmly approve our spirituality. There is scarcely a thought in our idle reveries that does not somehow shore up a sagging sense of worth.

This unsettling discovery becomes more disturbing when we notice that the sense of unworth motivates us even though we are conscious of its making us divided. Though we genuinely sympathize with a victim of parental abuse, we quite consciously enjoy congratulating ourselves for doing so. We may give words of encouragement to a faltering friend with unfeigned care, even though we are aware of the heightened feeling of importance that her grateful response brings. We might sincerely seek confession at church, but at the same time take conscious pleasure in the esteem we get from acquaintances there.

Our need for a sense of worth is so strong that we possess a deep fear of not having it. Ernest Becker calls this fear the "dread of insignificance."[9] Each of us, he says, has a "burning desire . . . to count, to make a difference on the planet." Each person is desperate to "stand

9. Becker, *Escape from Evil* (New York: Macmillan–The Free Press, 1975), p. 3.

out, be a hero, make the biggest possible contribution to world life, show that he *counts* more than anything or anyone else." This desire for cosmic significance "expresses the heart of the creature."[10] It leads us to erect monuments to ourselves, immerse ourselves in accepted cultural patterns, engage in activities that make us different from others, and identify with heroes. The dread is so intense, Becker says, that avoiding it is a matter of life and death. We would shrivel up if a sense of insignificance were to sweep over us.

This dread makes our efforts at self-justification exceedingly strong. We expend enormous amounts of energy in attempts to win the favor of others. We identify ourselves with our successes and pursue self-justifying projects with unrivaled intensity. We cling tenaciously to activities that we believe bring high regard. We put ourselves through extreme pain to achieve the success we know others admire. Our feelings of satisfaction with life are at their peak when we feel approved of by others.

Martin Luther once wrote that "there is no greater pain than the gnawing pangs of conscience."[11] This explains why we make such strenuous efforts to justify ourselves. Self-justification convinces us that the accusations of our conscience are mistaken. It soothes the sharp pain of being fully conscious of our real natures. It clothes our naked selves.

So intractable is this tendency that we engage in it to compensate for even the basest of activities. In Tolstoy's novel *Resurrection*, Maslova, a prostitute, feels no shame for her profession. On the contrary, she is pleased and almost proud of it because she views herself as an important and necessary person. She has the power to satisfy men's desires. They need her, and in this she finds her significance in life. Of Maslova's self-justification, Tolstoy asks, "How could it be otherwise?" revealing the power of her drive to justify herself.[12]

We can also use legitimate activities to justify ourselves. Our

10. Ibid., pp. 4, 3.

11. Luther, quoted by Merold Westphal in *God, Guilt, and Death: An Existential Phenomenology of Religion* (Bloomington: Indiana University Press, 1984), p. 110.

12. Tolstoy, *Resurrection*, trans. Rosemary Edmonds (New York: Penguin Books, 1966), p. 201.

jobs, for example, are particularly strong suppliers of self-justification. This is especially true of professional people, who are acutely conscious that their jobs are highly regarded by the rest of society. It is true too of ministers and counselors, who may constantly be aware of the love they give and the broken lives they help fix.

Our positions in society are also sources of justification. We compare our rank with that of others, and when we see that an acquaintance has a higher one, we immediately think that she has had special advantages in obtaining it, or that her place is not really desirable after all, or that our rank is higher than someone else's we know. We do the same with respect to our possessions. If we observe that a friend has an expensive car, house, or dress, we remind ourselves that we have things others would admire. It is as if our worth depends on what we own. Perhaps this is why Jesus observed that it is harder for a wealthy person to accept grace than it is for a camel to get through the low gate next to the main gate of a city (Matt. 19:24).

Nothing escapes our use when we attempt to obtain self-justification. Our clothes give us the feeling of being approved because they mark us as belonging to groups we want to be part of and distinguish us from groups we do not want to be part of. Our attractive faces and hairstyles make us feel valued because we know that people notice them. Our worthy character traits and sacrificial activities make us feel as if we stand above the crowd because such traits and activities are universally admired. We can even use our children and our parents as sources of self-justification. In their character traits and mere existence we find our value. So it is with the institutions with which we are affiliated, the colleges from which we have graduated, and the influential people we know. From well-kept lawns to books we write, from the attention we receive to the money we give — we use all these things to justify our existence to ourselves.

Others reinforce our drive for self-justification. Parents may convey to us that they will accept us only if we obtain good grades in school or only if we do well in competition. Society tells us that we have more worth if we own the right car, wear the right clothes, live in the right neighborhood, and are white, male, intelligent, and successful. Churches too sometimes reinforce the drive for self-justification: we are accepted only if we refrain from unapproved behavior. A subtle atmosphere of conditional acceptance may exist in a church even though it officially stands for love and grace.

There are a variety of distinctively religious methods of justifying ourselves. One common method is to think that God accepts us because we are not like certain members of secular society. We refrain from cheating, lying, and other questionable practices, and we exhibit Christian virtues that many in secular society do not. Another method involves believing the right things. We take pride in the fact that we believe what God has told us, including the truth that we are justified only by his grace. Still another method is to identify with a Christian group. Here our self-justification is based not on our belief that we have the truth but on our being part of a church or other Christian group. Although we may have a sense of personal sin, we also have a lively sense of corporate superiority when we identify with a Christian group.

Each of these methods is like the practice of the Pharisee, who justified himself before God on the grounds that he fasted twice a week, tithed, and was not greedy, dishonest, or guilty of adultery. He was a good, religious person, esteemed for his charity, uprightness, and knowledge of Scripture, doing all the right things and refraining from all the wrong ones. It is astonishing that he could have tricked himself into believing that God accepted him for these reasons. It is just as astonishing and even more unsettling when we discover ourselves doing exactly the same. We do all that we can to deny that we are.

There is an effective technique that we can use to uncover our self-justification. It is to remove the suspected sources of self-justification and see how we feel. If we were to give up our jobs, divest ourselves of our cherished possessions, renounce our superior social status, or wear dirty clothes in public, we would find out whether the foundation of our sense of worth is one of these or God's grace. We would have the same illumination if we were to fail in some significant way, for then we would discover whether it is success or grace in which we find our identity. Success and grace can exist side by side. But our tendency to use success as self-justification is so strong that it is good, perhaps even necessary, for us to fail periodically. That insures that success does not replace grace in our lives.

34

Comparison

Comparing ourselves to others is an especially attractive way of obtaining self-justification. Our aim when we compare is to think of ourselves as being as good as or better than others. We look for something in them that they cannot do as well, something they do not possess, or a native quality they do not have. Finding such features is easy. An acquaintance may be artistically creative, but, we instinctively think, we are better at sewing than she is. She may have well-known friends or a highly regarded job, but we have well-known friends and a highly regarded job too.

We also employ comparison when we make up ways of being superior to others. We may not be as good-looking or as smart as others, but we tell ourselves that we are even better-looking, even smarter. Our abilities may be average, but we convince ourselves that they are superior.

Most of our thoughts about other people consist of these kinds of comparisons. We ask, "Am I as good on the job as a coworker? Does a friend dress as well as I do? Am I more in touch with my feelings than my spouse? Is a neighbor as well-paid as I am?" We can scarcely make new acquaintances without trying to find out what they are like so we can see how we stand in comparison to them. If we are rich, we feel superior to the upper middle class. If we belong to the upper middle class, we feel superior to the lower middle class. If we belong to the lower middle class, we feel superior both to the poor for having more than they do, and to the upper middle class and the rich for *not* having wealth or a superior attitude.

Perhaps we have periods of solitude in which we contemplate the point of what we do and probe the depths of human experience. We are not like the masses, we tell ourselves, who dull their sensitivities to ultimate issues by watching television every evening or who unthinkingly rush along Jackson Street at 5:07 to catch the 5:18 train at Union Station. They are caught up in external forces, accept popular opinion at face value, and have no idea of what it is like to think for themselves. Those of us who spend time alone reading and thinking are particularly susceptible to making this kind of comparison.

Those of us who have a sense of mission about our jobs and a strong inner drive to work are susceptible to making a different kind of comparison. We like to think of ourselves as doing something significant with our lives, and we especially like to think that we do not waste spare time in frivolous activities. Unlike cashiers, assembly-line workers, and those who live only for the weekend, we are getting ahead. What *we* do counts.

Irvin Yalom tells of a time he caught himself making this kind of comparison. "I was taking a brief vacation alone at a Caribbean beach resort. One evening I was reading, and from time to time I glanced up to watch the bar boy who was doing nothing save languidly staring out to sea — much like a lizard sunning itself on a warm rock, I thought. The comparison I made between him and me made me feel very smug, very cozy. He was simply doing nothing — wasting time; I was, on the other hand, doing something useful, reading, learning. I was, in short, getting ahead."[13]

The most universal form of comparison comes from the sense of specialness we possess.[14] "I am me," each of us feels. "I am different from everyone else. I am somebody because I am who I am." We feel superior simply because we are we and they are they. It is no particular quality which makes us superior — just the fact that we exist and feel and move.

The pervasiveness of the sense of specialness can scarcely be overestimated. Though we rarely articulate this sense, it is present in nearly every waking moment, most of the time submerged but sometimes at the surface of consciousness. It is diffused through our thoughts as an awareness of uniqueness and personal importance.

This awareness turns into envy when we notice that someone else has a quality that we would like to have or has done something that we would like to have done. We resent the other's superiority because we take it as discrediting ourselves. To compensate, we think

13. Yalom, *Existential Psychotherapy,* p. 124. He continues, "All was well, until some internal imp asked the terrible question: Getting ahead of what? How? And (even worse) why?"

14. "Each of us, first as a child and then as an adult, clings to an irrational belief in our specialness" (Yalom, *Existential Psychotherapy,* p. 96).

of something we possess or do that is superior in some way, or we think of some inferiority in the other.

Comparison occurs in Christian contexts as well. When we notice other Christians exhibiting Christian virtues, we may secretly think of ourselves as being at least as good. We have spiritual attainments too and should be noticed for them. We read Christian books and ponder them, spend time with other Christians, pray, and in general do what good Christians should do.

Sometimes comparison takes the form of overt or covert criticism of other Christians. They are just average Christians, we tell ourselves, whereas we take our Christianity much more seriously. Some of them are not very active as Christians, some come to church mainly out of habit, and some conform to society's values more than a Christian should. Some Christians, in fact, may not be Christians at all. Fear of disapproval or self-justification may be making them think they have accepted God's forgiving love when in fact they have not. We, however, have had profound Christian experiences, by "profound" meaning not just "deep" but "beyond what most Christians have." We expect others to admire these experiences when we describe them. Nor do we consider it boastful or prideful when we talk about our profound experiences, because we publicly attribute them to God — forgetting that the Pharisee also attributed his being different from everyone else to God.[15]

If we cannot find a Christian virtue with which to make ourselves superior, we may find a vice into which we have sunk more deeply. We may think of ourselves as worse sinners than other Christians or as having been worse sinners before we became Christians, and thus, by a strange logic, think of ourselves as superior in a reverse way.

Moreover, we may believe ourselves to be better than those who are not Christians. We are accepted by God and they are not; we believe the Bible is God's Word and they do not; we have been made into new persons by God's grace and they have not. We love, and

---

15. Jonathan Edwards, *Treatise on Religious Affections* (New Haven: Yale University Press, 1959), p. 321. The Pharisee prayed, "I thank you, God, that I am not greedy, dishonest, or an adulterer, like everybody else" (Luke 18:11).

they are indifferent; we care about our eternal destiny, and they are unconcerned; we have inner peace, but they have anxiety and pain. "Who can do good things," Thomas Merton asks, "without seeking to taste in them some sweet distinction from the common run of sinners in this world?"[16]

We are tempted to compare ourselves with other Christians and with non-Christians *because* we take our Christianity seriously.[17] We want to be different, to be lights for Christ, because that is what the Bible tells us to be. We strive to grow more mature in Christ, becoming less and less like those disapproved of in the Bible: the Pharisee, the worldly person, the gossiper, the builder of bigger barns. We are acutely aware of the sharp contrast that Christianity draws between good and evil. We are conscious of the cosmic drama of which we are a part, a drama in which ultimately we sheep will be separated from those goats.

All of these differences between us and "them" may be true. Eliminating comparisons does not require denying differences. What it requires is not thinking of the differences, for once we let them slip into our minds, we almost invariably use them for self-justification. It also requires not thinking that we refrain from making comparisons, for we may unwittingly compare ourselves to those who do make comparisons.

Perhaps, too, eliminating comparisons requires confessing our sins to those whom we think of as sinners. There may not be quite as much difference between ourselves and them as we think. We may in fact be no different even though we think we are far different. This is what Dostoyevsky conveyed in one of the sermons of Father Zossima, a Russian monk, in *The Brothers Karamasov:* "Remember particularly that you cannot be a judge of anyone. For there can be no judge of a felon on earth, until the judge himself recognizes that he is just such a felon as the man standing before him."[18]

16. Merton, *New Seeds of Contemplation* (1961; rpt. New York: New Directions, 1972), p. 49.

17. The one "who is anxious to do his Christian duty, in contrast to the lifeless and indifferent, will be all the more prone to compare himself with others to their disadvantage and his own glory" (John F. Smith, in the editor's introduction to Edwards's *Treatise on Religious Affections,* p. 36).

18. Dostoyevsky, *The Brothers Karamazov,* p. 378.

Comparing is an especially strong obstructor of singleness of heart. Besides playing a part in self-justification, it occupies our minds and crowds out God's concerns. Because of it, we cannot focus our attention on molding ourselves into persons who love and care, who treat others gently, who exhibit patience, kindness, and interest in others' welfare. Comparing motivates our life projects — what we do, say, wear, and possess — and directs our energy toward producing favorable impressions on others. We act for the sake of these impressions and thereby think of people simply as means for getting admiration. We cannot listen when others tell us about their activities, thoughts, or troubles, for our minds are constantly comparing what we hear with something in our own lives. We cannot empathize with others' inner wounds because comparing prevents us from identifying with them. Nor can we sincerely admire the good qualities of acquaintances or give them praise and encouragement because comparing causes us to depreciate those qualities.

Self-congratulation

Another way we justify ourselves is to commend ourselves for what we do. When we do so, we are engaging in self-congratulation.

Self-congratulation sometimes occurs in fairly conscious ways, with an inner "You were very loving with _____ yesterday" or "You offered a good prayer in church today." At other times it occurs less consciously, with the vague feeling that we are the ones who have loved or that we have prayed well.

We can engage in self-congratulation even if we act single-mindedly in other respects. We might love without anticipation of return, yet be moved by the thought that we have loved and that we have given ourselves to another. We might profess belief in Christ because we genuinely want to, not because we fear disapproval if we do not, yet at the same time admire ourselves for having the belief.

We engage in one form of self-congratulation when we feel indispensable. We may undertake projects, seize opportunities, and volunteer for tasks that others avoid, imagining that without us

39

nothing would get done. We may think that others depend on us and could not survive if we were absent. If we recoil from the thought that someone else can do something that we thought only we could do, we are likely to be commending ourselves for our indispensability.

We also engage in self-congratulation when we act for the sake of an otherwise justifiable self-respect: we do things because we want to acknowledge an achievement to ourselves or to have a sense of doing well. Realizing that we have done well is legitimate, and having self-respect is too, but when we act solely because we want to have the realization and the respect, we are acting from a further motive. Loving for the sake of loving while at the same time having the sense of loving well is one thing; loving because we want to have this sense is another. We would be using someone for our own gain if we loved that person in this second way. And we ourselves would feel used if we knew someone was loving us in this way.

Sometimes self-congratulation becomes exaggerated and turns into inordinate self-esteem. We tell ourselves that we are good workers, better than others, or that we are nice to people, nicer than most. We make an internal ostentatious display of our goodness, observed and enjoyed only by ourselves. But it spills over on occasion and is noticed by others.

One subtle and nearly universal way in which we congratulate ourselves is by taking pleasure in our thoughts. They are ours, and that is reason enough to be proud of them. The same is true for things we do. The mere fact that we do them makes us esteem them.

Self-congratulation operates especially subtly in Christian contexts. The temptation to praise ourselves for acting in conformity with accepted Christian standards is nearly undetectable. So is the temptation to praise ourselves for praying daily, singing hymns enthusiastically, and reading the Bible regularly. It is the same for believing correct Christian doctrine and for having changed dramatically upon becoming a Christian.

We can congratulate ourselves even for the very things that are most incompatible with self-congratulation. It is important to be in a right relation with God, so important, we feel, that we may admire ourselves when we get into that relation. We have done something significant, we might think, after having confessed and repented. "Even a humble enduring of poverty may signify more devotion to the humility of the endurer than to the bounty of the Giver of want."[19]

What we get from congratulating ourselves is warm, gratifying pride. The power of this feeling can scarcely be overestimated. For its sake we love those who need special attention, do things that we believe will make a difference in others' lives, and adopt beliefs that we conceive to be crucial for a right standing with God. Even if no one else notices what we do, *we* notice.

One of the dangers of self-congratulation is that we will think God admires us for the same reasons that we admire ourselves. We tend to imagine God having the same attitude toward us that we have toward ourselves. If we think we are not worth much, we will imagine God thinking the same. If we admire ourselves for being good Christians, loving humbly, and giving encouragement to the downcast, we will conceive of God admiring us for these too.

Jonathan Edwards noticed this connection between self-admiration and the thought that God admires us. He writes, "He that is proud of his experiences, arrogates something to himself, as though his experience were some dignity of his. And if he looks on them as his own dignity, he necessarily thinks that God looks on 'em so too; for he necessarily thinks his own opinion of 'em to be true; and consequently judges that God looks on them as he does; and so unavoidably imagines that God looks on his experiences as a dignity in him, as he looks on 'em himself; and that he glisters as much in God's eyes, as he does in his own."[20] The danger here, as Edwards must have realized, is that our relishing of God's admiration squeezes out the desire for God's grace.

It is important to distinguish between God's admiring us and his being pleased with us because he made us. Genesis 1 says that when God made us, he was pleased with what he saw. He was pleased, no doubt, because what he had made was good. Now if

19. Louis MacKay, *Kierkegaard: A Kind of Poet* (Philadelphia: University of Pennsylvania Press, 1971), p. 98.
20. Edwards, *Treatise on Religious Affections,* p. 318.

God has this attitude toward us, it is legitimate for us to have it toward ourselves. We are good because God made us. This legitimate self-regard differs from the self-congratulation that squeezes out the desire for grace. Legitimate self-regard is based on God's making us good, and we can have it without undercutting the desire to be loved and forgiven. (Indeed, it is good to have this self-regard in order to counteract self-loathing.) Because self-congratulation is different from this self-regard, its opposite is not self-loathing or self-abnegation, as it is for self-regard. The opposite of self-congratulation is, rather, self-forgetfulness.

Forgetting is defined as "treating with inattention or disregard, putting out of mind." To forget ourselves, then, is to become unmindful of ourselves. Jesus referred to self-forgetfulness when he said in Matthew 16:24 that we must deny ourselves if we want to follow him. The idea is conveyed more explicitly in the Today's English Version translation of this verse: "If anyone wants to come with me, he must forget himself, carry his cross, and follow me."

The servants who said "We have done only what we ought to have done" (Luke 17:10) are exemplars of those with self-forgetfulness. They do not take pride that they have done what their employers have told them to do. They care not that they are the ones who have loved unlovable outcasts, that they have encouraged those who have given up hope, or that they have saved acquaintances from lethal despair. They are not conscious of having served faithfully, of having given more money than they can afford, or of having salved friends' wounds. They have given themselves away and do not know it.

Those who forget themselves must, of course, also forget that they are doing so. For once the thought that they are forgetting themselves slips into their consciousness, they are liable to congratulate themselves for it.

Self-forgetfulness, it should be noted, is not just disregarding ourselves; it is also focusing attention on something outside us. When, for instance, we lose ourselves in some activity, we become oblivious to ourselves, and our entire consciousness is directed toward what we are doing. The same is true when we identify with someone else's feelings; we forget our own and are aware only of the other person's. Worship works in the same way, and so does gratitude for God's love. Self-forgetful gratitude has God as its object, not the gratitude itself. Once the gratitude becomes the focus of attention, the temptation to congratulate ourselves arises.

In "Love Hides the Multiplicity of Sins," Kierkegaard notes the connection between self-forgetfulness and focusing attention on others. "He who in love forgets himself, forgets his sufferings in order to think of another's, forgets all his wretchedness in order to think of another's, forgets what he himself loses in order lovingly to consider another's loss, forgets his advantage in order lovingly to look after another's advantage." On the other hand, Kierkegaard continues, "the self-lover is busy; he shouts and complains and insists on his rights in order to make sure he is not forgotten."[21]

The self-forgetful person, Kierkegaard tells us, thinks of the sufferings of others, their troubles and pains, and their struggles and losses. She rejoices in their joys and delights in their virtues and accomplishments. She does not insist that people notice her, nor does she insist that she notice herself. Her noticing is centered elsewhere.

*   *   *

Giving up our self-congratulating and comparing is painful and difficult. We have pursued self-justification so thoroughly and intensely that the transition from it to grace's justification fractures our deep-seated habits and conceptions of who we are. Tolstoy's Maslova eventually saw all this. Though for years she used her vocation as a means to justify herself, she finally saw through her flattering scheme. However, she was not then ready to accept grace. So she saturated herself with vodka to block out the painful revelation that had come to her. Not until later could she face herself more squarely, and then she wept over her ruined life.[22]

Our whole lives, from the minutest details to the grandest projects, are efforts to justify ourselves. Only when we realize the bankruptcy of these efforts are we ready to receive grace.

21. Kierkegaard, *Works of Love,* trans. Howard V. Hong and Edna H. Hong (New York: Harper, 1962), p. 262.
22. Tolstoy, *Resurrection,* pp. 220, 321.

Receiving grace is immensely liberating. When the consciousness that God unreservedly accepts us remains in the forefront of
our minds, the need to use our actions to justify ourselves is squeezed
out. We are not driven by the craving to secure our worth by
impressing others. We are released from anxiety about whether we
are successful in our attempts to obtain validation. We cease being
preoccupied with the thought that maybe others do not approve of
us. We become freed from the insatiable and irresistible impulse to
seek others' esteem. Grace liberates us from our apprehensive and
uneasy striving to vindicate ourselves.

The Impulse to Live Outside Ourselves

Dividedness also occurs in what can be called "living outside ourselves." When we live outside ourselves, we identify with some group
— the "crowd," as Kierkegaard puts it — and lose ourselves in it.
We become oblivious to ourselves, forgetting that we are distinct
persons. This oblivion is not the self-forgetfulness of unselfish caring;
it is the oblivion of lost identity. We become absorbed in the other,
losing consciousness of our individuality. The beliefs and desires that
we think are ours really belong to the group. Here the dividedness
consists of being something different from what we appear to be.
We appear to be individuals who have their own internal substance,
but we are really "group persons" with hollow insides.

Consider two examples. Imagine that a rather unexcitable person goes to a baseball game at which the crowd responds with wild
delight whenever the home team scores. The infectious enthusiasm
rubs off, and she too cheers. Or imagine that a person with little
political passion finds herself in a demonstration or at a rally. Without
consciously choosing to do so, she chants with the chanters, yells
with the yellers, and in general is caught up in the emotional intensity
of the moment.

In each case the person loses herself in others so thoroughly
that their thought patterns, feelings, and ways of acting become hers,
or — what amounts to the same thing — hers become theirs. She
does not have a conscious awareness of herself as being different

from the others. She does, of course, think of herself as being different in certain ways. But she does not have this sense of separateness at the times she is seized by the crowd's response.

The same occurs with young children who have not yet separated themselves from their parents and with adult children who still obtain their sense of identity from their parents. In a similar way, we sometimes uncritically immerse ourselves in our profession or in allegiance to our country, unconsciously internalizing its reputation and values. On occasion this also happens with respect to individuals — persons whom we imitate in certain ways without knowing that we are doing so. In all of these cases, the words we utter, the beliefs we have, even the feelings we experience are someone else's.

Something like this "being caught in the crowd" also occurs in Christian contexts. The general atmosphere in a church, the emotional tone, the belief system — we can take in all of these things unconsciously. Although our resulting beliefs, feelings, and responses appear to others and to ourselves to be our own, they are not.

We see clearly how we have become identified with a Christian group when we undergo the "wake up" phenomenon. This occurs when we first realize our identity has been lost. While it is lost, we are unaware of the fact. But when we begin to see what has been going on, we discover that what we have taken to be our love of God has really been the church's love. We become aware that what we thought was our own openness to God's grace has really been others' and that we ourselves have never been in such a state. Of course, if these others are also living outside themselves, then it would be not their actual openness to grace with which we would be identifying but what we take to be their openness. And they too would be identifying with what they take to be our openness. They would be just as empty as we are.

A number of writers have described this phenomenon of living outside ourselves. Kierkegaard says that when it occurs, there is an immediate connection between us and others. Because of this connection, our actions and feelings are passive, which means that they happen to us instead of originating from us. "The self is bound up in immediacy with the other in desiring, craving, enjoying, etc., yet passively." Such a self is not really itself, Kierkegaard notes. "The man of immediacy . . . wishes to be someone else." In fact, this self does not recognize itself except by external characteristics that it shares with others; it has no inner substance. "The man of immediacy does not know himself, he quite literally identifies himself only by the clothes he wears, he identifies having a self by externalities."[23]

Kierkegaard means for his analysis to apply not just to identification with society at large but to identification with Christian groups. He thinks that the same phenomenon which occurs in secular social contexts also occurs in churches. "In Christendom he [the man of immediacy] is also a Christian, goes to church every Sunday, listens to and understands the parson, indeed, they have a mutual understanding."[24] Kierkegaard is not talking about the occasional Christian, the one who only nominally identifies with Christianity. He is talking about the one who is an active participant, the one who attends church regularly and listens to the sermons. If such a person has uncritically identified with those in the church, he is nothing more than a copy of them. He thinks he has vital Christian emotions — sorrow for sin, gratitude for God's grace, and outgoing love. What he really has is other people's sorrow, gratitude, and love, or what he takes to be their sorrow, gratitude, and love. He is not himself, but is a crowd Christian, having adopted others' Christianity in a secondhand way.

José Ortega y Gasset, a Spanish philosopher, describes the individual who lives outside himself as being estranged from himself. Such an individual is pure otherness: he lives not from himself but from what is other than himself.[25] Max Scheler, a German philosopher, says that the person who has identified himself with another is unaware of his individual identity as distinct from that of the other. There is "a total submergence of one person's consciousness in another's." When this happens, the person's spiritual independence is paralyzed. He is disabled as a spiritual personality, abandons his

23. Kierkegaard, *The Sickness unto Death,* trans. Howard V. Hong and Edna H. Hong (Princeton: Princeton University Press, 1980), pp. 51, 53.

24. Kierkegaard, *The Sickness unto Death,* p. 52.

25. Ortega y Gasset, cited in *Phenomenology and Existentialism,* ed. Richard M. Zaner and Don Ihde (New York: Putnam, 1973), pp. 217, 218.

spiritual dignity, and "allows his instinctive life to look after itself."[26] Irvin Yalom, an American psychiatrist, writes that in merging with a larger group, there is no separate "I." One loses self-awareness; selfhood is fused into the group.[27]

The impulse to live outside ourselves comes from a number of sources. Contagion is one. It acts on us almost automatically, and often we must consciously resist to avoid passively adopting the emotions of a group. Plato gives a vivid description of the power of contagion. The public, he has Socrates say in *The Republic*, trains up "young and old, men and women alike, into the most accomplished specimens of the character it desires to produce." It does so "whenever the populace crowds together at any public gathering, in the Assembly, the law-courts, the theatre, or the camp, and sits there clamouring its approval or disapproval, both alike excessive, of whatever is being said or done; booing and clapping till the rocks ring and the whole place redoubles the noise of their applause and outcries. In such a scene what do you suppose will be a young man's state of mind? What sort of private instruction will have given him the strength to hold out against the force of such a torrent, or will save him from being swept away down the stream, until he accepts all their notions of right and wrong, does as they do, and comes to be just such a man as they are?"[28]

People in churches do not, of course, boo and clap or clamor their approval and disapproval. Their applause and outcries are a good deal more subtle than what occurs in a stadium. But these responses do occur in churches, nevertheless, and we hear them. The question here is not the rightness or wrongness of what churches make noise about. The question is whether their responses will carry us to grace or whether we will experience it on our own.

Christian virtues can of course originate inside us even though

26. Scheler, *The Nature of Sympathy,* trans. Peter Heath (Hamden, Conn.: Shoestring Press–Archon Books, 1973), pp. 35, 36. See also Philip Mercer, *Sympathy and Ethics* (New York: Oxford University Press, 1972), pp. 14, 15.

27. Yalom, *Existential Psychotherapy*, p. 380.

28. Plato, *The Republic,* trans. Francis M. Cornford (New York: Oxford University Press, 1945), p. 199, 492B.

they are stimulated by associating with others. Being with a Christian group does not automatically mean we will lose ourselves in it. In fact, being with those who are generous and compassionate is a good way to incite these virtues in us. To avoid becoming external persons, however, we must distinguish between consciously allowing ourselves to be encouraged and unconsciously allowing ourselves to be taken over by others. In the former we are genuinely ourselves, but in the latter we are really someone else.

Another source of the impulse to live outside ourselves is fear of isolation. "The most terrifying burden of the creature is to be isolated," writes Ernest Becker.[29] "To be like everyone else . . . saves one from the isolation of selfhood," Irvin Yalom claims.[30] This fear begins early and travels with us through life. It is alleviated not just by associating with a group but by adopting the power of the group as our own. Becker says, "Each child grounds himself in some power that transcends him. Usually it is a combination of his parents, his social group, and the symbols of his society and nation. This is the unthinking web of support which allows him to believe in himself, as he functions on the automatic security of delegated powers."[31] What allows the child, and subsequently the adult, to feel confident is that "he lives on borrowed powers"; he is "embedded in a web of someone else's power."[32]

This fear of isolation is more than simply the fear of being alone and separated from a group. It is also the fear of believing for oneself, of acting on one's own, and of adopting one's own stance toward life, all of which are a kind of isolation because they involve being individual. Kierkegaard makes this point when he says that we fear risking "something on our own" more than we fear death.[33] The

29. Becker, *The Denial of Death* (New York: Macmillan–The Free Press, 1973), p. 171.

30. Yalom, *Existential Psychotherapy,* p. 381.

31. Becker, *The Denial of Death,* p. 89.

32. Ibid.

33. "For even more than death the individual fears the judgment and protest of reflection upon his wishing to risk something on his own" (Kierkegaard, *The Present Age,* trans. Alexander Dru, in *A Kierkegaard Anthology,* ed. Robert Bretall [New York: Random House–The Modern Library, 1946], p. 261).

person who has this kind of fear and who forgets himself in a multitude "does not dare to believe in himself, finds it too hazardous to be himself and far easier and safer to be like the others, to become a copy, a number, a mass man."[34]

We use Christian groups to assuage the fear of isolation in the same way that we use parents, friends, and social groups to assuage it. Letting a Christian group live our Christianity for us "gives us a feeling of security and has something tranquilizing about it," Kierkegaard observes.[35] We protect ourselves from the dreaded feeling of being left out. We also relieve ourselves of the burden and the risk of dealing with God on our own.

Another source of living outside ourselves is the desire to run from God. When we unconsciously hide within a group's Christianity, we may really be doing so in order to shield ourselves from God's gaze — we do not want him knowing what we are really like. Or we may be telling God that we do not need him; the group's Christianity is what makes us feel that our existence is good enough.[36] In both of these, the shielding and the illusion of goodness, we use the very group that for us may have provided the path to God in order to flee from God.

We are also incited to live outside ourselves by the desire to obtain a sense of power. When we identify with a group, we imagine ourselves having some of the power that we perceive the group to have. Identifying with our nation, for example, gives us the feeling of having the same superior strength we conceive it to have, especially during a time of war. The same is true when we identify with particular churches or with the Christian church in general. The Christian church has a certain kind of power, we observe, partly because it shows us how to justify our existence. We can share in

---

34. Kierkegaard, *The Sickness unto Death*, pp. 33-34.

35. Kierkegaard, quoted by Liselotte Richter in "Kierkegaard's Position in his Religio-Sociological Situation," in *A Kierkegaard Critique,* ed. Howard A. Johnson and Niels Thulstrup (New York: Harper, 1962), p. 60.

36. "'Being good' can be a form of defiance, a way of telling God that I need no help to become what I should be" (C. Stephen Evans, *Søren Kierkegaard's Christian Psychology* [Grand Rapids, Mich.: Zondervan Publishing Co., 1990], p. 58).

this power by losing ourselves in the church. In doing so we gain the appearance of being something we are not.

Erich Fromm, an American psychoanalyst and social philosopher, describes how this illusion arises. "If, for reasons of weakness, anxiety, incompetence, etc., man is not able to *act,* if he is impotent, he suffers. . . . Man cannot accept the state of complete powerlessness without attempting to restore his capacity to act. But can he, and how? One way is to submit to and identify with a person or group having power. By this symbolic participation in another person's life, man has the illusion of acting, when in reality he only submits to and becomes a part of those who act."[37]

The opposite of living outside ourselves is what Kierkegaard calls being an individual.[38] When we live as individuals, our actions, beliefs, and desires come from ourselves; our enthusiasm and contrition are ours and not the group's. The tax collector's prayer is our own and not someone else's. When we enter the sanctuary, we do so as if no one else is there (though, at the same time, we do so desiring to be with others). Our love springs from our own spontaneous overflow.

Mutual Expectations

So far I have described the sources of dividedness as coming from our own motives. It is our reward-seeking and our fear of disapproval that make us different from what we appear to be. Now I must point out that other people's rewards and disapproval contribute to our dividedness. Dividedness has both a personal and a social source; it comes from our desire for rewards and from others' giving of rewards.

The acceptance others give us, for example, is a reward. Because

---

37. Fromm, *The Heart of Man* (New York: Harper, 1964), p. 31.

38. "The most ruinous evasion of all is to be hidden in the crowd in an attempt to escape God's supervision of him as an individual, in an attempt to get away from hearing God's voice as an individual" (Kierkegaard, *Purity of Heart Is to Will One Thing,* p. 185).

it is based largely on our successful performance, we, knowing that this is so, strive to be successful in ways that we think will garner this acceptance. This is particularly true when both we and those with whom we associate are Christians. Christians expect other Christians to be virtuous, to do the kinds of things the Bible requires of Christians, and to display devoutness — not ostentatiously, of course, but genuinely. When these expectations are not met, acceptance tends to decrease.

Expectations are often coupled with disapproval. Because Christians tend to express strong disapproval of certain kinds of shortcomings, we are pushed (if we are also Christians) to appear virtuous when in their presence. Being in their presence encourages us to hide our deficiencies, to keep our struggles to ourselves, and to display our Christian goodness. Doing these things not only decreases the likelihood that other Christians will show disapproval toward us; it also increases the validation we feel for our lives. Other Christians' expectations and approval thus incite us to engage in self-justification.

The comparisons others make cause us to make comparisons too. The distinctions they make with respect to social success and wealth rub off on us, as do the distinctions Christians make with respect to devoutness, church activity, and conformity to Christian standards.

Our sense of worth, as well, is maintained by countless specific contacts with others. Their approval of what we do, our smooth interaction with them, their giving us gifts and flattering recognition — all contribute to the significance we conceive ourselves to have. Having a secure place in a family, a church, a workplace, fitting into a social network, participating in a common effort at work or church — these supply us with generous doses of significance. Even a "Hello" from someone who smiles at us and uses our name contributes; it is not just a friendly greeting but is, we feel, an affirmation of our very existence. Simply being with others gives us a sense of worth. As Kierkegaard noted, "No one wants to be an individual existing human being. . . . Just as in the desert individuals must travel in large caravans out of fear of robbers and wild animals, so individuals today have a horror of existence . . . ; they dare to live only in great herds and cling together *en masse* in order to be at least something."[39]

Whenever we are part of a group, those in the group expect us to fit into certain roles. We know that we can obtain a sense of worth by fitting into or appearing to fit into these roles, and so we do. Put differently, others expect us to play at being what we are, and because we find this expectation nearly impossible to resist, we act out our lives.

The philosopher Jean-Paul Sartre gives an example of how this game-playing works. "Let us consider," he writes, "this waiter in the cafe. His movement is quick and forward, a little too precise, a little too rapid. He comes toward the patrons with a step a little too quick. He bends forward a little too eagerly; his voice, his eyes express an interest a little too solicitous for the order of the customer. Finally there he returns, trying to imitate in his walk the inflexible stiffness of some kind of automaton while carrying his tray with the reckless-ness of a tight-rope-walker by putting it in a perpetually unstable, perpetually broken equilibrium which he perpetually reestablishes by a light movement of the arm and hand. All his behavior seems to us a game. . . . But what is he playing? We need not watch long before we can explain it: he is playing *at being* a waiter in a cafe."[40]

What is true of the waiter is true of others who perform services. "Their condition," continues Sartre, "is wholly one of ceremony." And why? — Because "the public demands of them that they realize it as a ceremony. . . . A grocer who dreams is offensive to the buyer, because such a grocer is not wholly a grocer. Society demands that he limit himself to his function as a grocer."[41]

The demand upon Christians to live as if in a continuous ceremony is no less than the demand upon grocers to function as grocers. We Christians tend to forget that the same pressures and

---

39. Kierkegaard, *Concluding Unscientific Postscript to Philosophical Fragments,* vol. 1, ed. and trans. Howard V. Hong and Edna H. Hong (Princeton: Princeton University Press, 1992), pp. 355-56.

40. Sartre, *Being and Nothingness,* trans. Hazel Barnes (New York: Philosophical Library, 1956), p. 59.

41. Ibid.

expectations that exist in secular social groups also exist within churches and other Christian groups. These pressures include normal social demands, such as that we dress in such and such a way to be acceptable or associate only with those of a similar economic status. They also include the demand that we act in certain religious ways, use certain words and phrases, even have certain facial expressions in order to fit the role of being a Christian. Silence regarding dividedness makes it seem that dividedness is nonexistent in Christians, and this causes us to deny or overlook it. An atmosphere of cheeriness, though infectious, does the same. We cannot admit that we have impulses to be important without disrupting the official picture of what Christians should be. A Christian who dreams is offensive to other Christians.

Clearly, then, other people contribute to our ambivalence and illusion. But there is more to the story. We are others to other people, so we contribute to their ambivalence and illusion just as much as they contribute to ours. All the things they do that undermine our singleness are things we do that undermine theirs. The crowd, which we tend to point our finger at with condescension, is not an impersonal other. We are part of it. Our first realization of this fact comes with an unsettling jolt. We instinctively notice what other people do to us but do not see what we do to them.

Consider the sense of worth again. My acquaintances obtain their sense of worth from me. My approval of them and friendly "Hello's" are affirmations, they feel, of their existence. Their contacts with me add to their sense of significance. They shrink from my disapproval and eagerly accept the rewards I give them.

Moreover, I incite in them the motives that undermine singleness of heart. My admiration of successful performance causes them to use their success as self-justification. My expectations that they act in Christian ways motivate them to use their Christian virtues to get approval from me. They hide their struggles with the Christian life because of these expectations and strive to appear virtuous to obtain my admiration. The comparisons I make infect their thinking; when I rank some Christians as better than others, they think of themselves as being in the better group. They play at being Christians because that is what I expect them to be. If they were to dream, I would be uncomfortable with them.

I am, then, as much a source of dividedness for others as they are for me. They are driven by the same motives that drive me, and they need me to satisfy these motives as much as I need them.

I am not an exception to these facts about dividedness just because I belong to a genuinely Christian church. (I want to think I am an exception for this reason, and I also want to think of my church as an exception.) I am not an exception just because I am a genuine Christian. (I want to think so for this reason too.) And I am not an exception just because I am I. I am enmeshed in all this just as much as the others whose motives I analyze, and they are enmeshed in it just as much as I am.

Chapter 4

Barriers to Singleness of Heart

Humankind cannot bear very much reality.

T. S. Eliot, *Four Quartets*

In every man there is something which to a certain degree prevents him from becoming perfectly transparent to himself; and this may be the case in so high a degree, he may be so inexplicably woven into relationships of life which extend far beyond himself, that he almost cannot reveal himself. But he who cannot reveal himself cannot love, and he who cannot love is the most unhappy man of all.

Kierkegaard, *Either/Or*

Singleness of heart gets lost in ways that operate independently of the motives described in the last chapter. Imagination tempts us to mistake imaginary love for real love. Busyness distracts us from single-minded pursuit of love. Indifference keeps us from caring about this pursuit, and resistance makes us oppose it.

Imagination

We spend much of our thought life imagining other people admiring us. We imagine ourselves being the hero who is acclaimed or the clever solver of problems. In Christian contexts we imagine ourselves being admired for our spirituality, our reliable participation in church activities, and our friendliness to difficult people. We also imagine ourselves actually being spiritual, reliable, and friendly. These qualities are attractive, and we like to think of ourselves as having them. So our imaginings contain two elements that are mixed together: images of others' admiration and images of our being good, spiritual, and loving.

Both in periods of quiet contemplation and in fleeting moments throughout the day, we experience these two elements. We picture ourselves giving a dollar to a street beggar in the presence of a friend who observes us doing it. We envision ourselves being sensitive to the depression, grief, and hardships of our friends, receiving appreciation for our words of encouragement. We imagine ourselves having inner peace and spiritual calm, surrounded by other Christians who notice our quiet radiance.

The image of obtaining admiration is a strong incentive for us to act compassionately and lovingly. So also is the image of actually being compassionate and loving. We often need this second kind of image to move us to action. If we picture ourselves talking gently to someone who has been annoying, we may actually talk gently to that person. If we imagine ourselves trusting God more deeply, we may be moved to do so.

It is desirable, then, for us to have images of ourselves being loving. What happens, however, is that we withdraw into them and mistake them for real loving. We think of ourselves as actually talking gently to an annoying person or trusting God deeply simply because we picture ourselves doing so. The temptation to mistake image for reality is intense because we really want to be gentle and trusting. Moreover, the image is much safer than the reality. Imaginary compassion is clean and tidy, but real compassion is often dirty and messy. An imaginary beggar does not stink; a real beggar does. Imaginary consolation involves no trauma; real consolation does.

Imaginary forgiveness does not hurt; real forgiveness does. Imaginary love is soothing and comfortable, but "active love is something severe and terrifying."[1]

Dostoyevsky recognized this disparity between imaginary love and real love in his novel entitled *The Brothers Karamazov*. In this story, one of the characters, a doctor, says, "The more I love humanity in general, the less I love men in particular, I mean, separately, as separate individuals. In my dreams, I am very often passionately determined to serve humanity, and I might quite likely have sacrificed my life for my fellow-creatures, if for some reason it had been suddenly demanded of me, and yet I'm quite incapable of living with anyone in one room for two days together, and I know that from experience."[2] Later, another character in the novel says, "To love a man, it's necessary that he should be hidden, for as soon as he shows his face, love is gone. Beggars, especially honorable beggars, should never show themselves in the streets, but ask for charity through the newspapers. Theoretically it is still possible to love one's neighbors, and sometimes even from a distance, but at close quarters almost never."[3]

In our dreams, as the doctor discovered, we have a high degree of earnestness. Our compassion is stirring, our vision of love and harmony is vivid, and our hearts are wounded by the thought of suffering humanity. We give gifts with deep feeling and touch the lonely and depressed with sympathetic hands. We have a sure and undoubting faith; our reception of God's grace is untainted by self-justification; we engage in Christian activities with a lively and eager interest. Our dream world, in sum, is one of "billowing inner energy."[4]

Sophia Tolstoy noticed this fact about her own dream world. In 1875, when she was 31, she observed in her diary entry for October 12, "On days like today I feel I am living in a dream. But

1. Fyodor Dostoyevsky, *The Brothers Karamazov*, trans. David Magarshack (New York: Penguin Books, 1958), p. 63.

2. Ibid., p. 62.

3. Ibid., pp. 276-77.

4. Ernest Becker, *The Denial of Death* (New York: Macmillan–The Free Press, 1973), p. 78.

no, this is life, not a dream. In dreams I go to vespers and pray as I never pray in real life, or else see the most marvellous flowers, or picture galleries, or crowds of people whom I neither hate nor avoid but love with my whole heart."[5]

Some of our dreams work themselves into reality, but some we mistakenly think of as being part of our true selves. We perceive ourselves to be exemplary Christians because we imagine ourselves so. We think we are alive to God because we picture that we are. "Quite often," Leo Tolstoy writes of himself in *Confession,* "a man goes on for years imagining that the religious teaching that had been imparted to him since childhood is still intact, while all the time there is not a trace of it left in him."[6]

The retreat into imagination becomes especially alluring when we develop an aversion to exerting the energy required for Christian living. When the strenuousness of such living becomes too much, we find it more comfortable simply to imagine ourselves engaging in it. We like the ease that imagination brings.[7]

How can we counteract the temptation to mistake images for reality? The first thing we can do is to catch ourselves dreaming. This involves being attentive to what goes on inside us and recognizing dreams for what they are. When we find we have withdrawn into them, we can tell ourselves, "This is imaginary love."

A second thing we can do is to put ourselves into situations we know will shake us loose from the safety of dream love. We can stand in front of the beggar, listen to his hopeless words, and smell his unwashed clothes. We can feel the sorrow of a widow, hear the complaints of those unjustly discriminated against, and listen to the pain of self-rejection of the suicidal. We can search the faces of the lonely, notice the anger and guilt feelings of an incest victim, and observe the frustration of women who have been unwillingly dom-

5. Tolstoy, *The Diaries of Sophia Tolstoy,* trans. Cathy Porter (New York: Random House, 1985), p. 51.

6. Tolstoy, *Confession,* trans. David Patterson (New York: W. W. Norton, 1983), p. 15.

7. "The lazy man always has a disproportionate power of imagination" (Søren Kierkegaard, *Purity of Heart Is to Will One Thing,* trans. Douglas V. Steere [New York: Harper, 1956], p. 116).

inated by men. We can sit in an alley with homeless alcoholics, walk the streets of gang-infested territory, look at the ramshackle housing of the involuntary poor, and read letters from a prisoner who writes of inhumane prison conditions. Doing these pulls us from our dreams and pushes us into active caring.

A third thing we can do is to dream deliberately and consciously with the aim of translating what we dream into reality. Doing this involves imagining how other people feel, reconstructing their situations, and picturing ourselves interacting with them. It means creatively conceiving of various responses we might make to another's distress. It also means transforming what we imagine into a vision of how we want actually to be instead of something we want to retreat to. It requires that we resist the enticement to shelter ourselves in the dream and substitute it for reality.

Busyness

In his perceptive book entitled *The Way of the Heart,* Henri Nouwen writes, "We move through life in such a distracted way that we do not even take the time and rest to wonder if any of the things we think, say, or do are *worth* thinking, saying, or doing."[8] What Nouwen has noticed is the extraordinary amount of busyness we engage in — activity that diverts our attention from the single-minded pursuit of eternity.

We do not want to know about busyness. Because we are Christians, we take pride in being among those who of all people have reflected on where they are going in life. We think that we are different from the general run of humanity and thus that we are exempt from Nouwen's observation. We resist taking an inventory of our time because we are afraid of discovering how much consists of distracting activities and how little consists of unhurried meditation. We especially resist the thought that our Christian activities may themselves divert us from eternity.

It is easy to be busy. We are active and restless creatures; we

8. Nouwen, *The Way of the Heart* (New York: Ballantine Books, 1981), p. 10.

must always be doing something. Few of us can sit still for long — we must be up and on to our next task. Our minds too are active and restless. They must always be thinking something; rarely do they become quiet.

It is easy to be busy, too, because everyone else is busy. We assume that the natural human state is to be doing things because we are surrounded with constant movement — energetic coworkers, traffic, fleeting images on the television screen, church services that must move along. We hear from the pulpit that it is action, not just words, that Christ calls us to, and though this is true, it makes us think that we continually have to be doing things to be good Christians. It scarcely occurs to us that there might be a different conception of what life or Christianity is about. We let our culture's or our church's busyness rub off on us without noticing that we are doing so.

Besides being easy, busyness is alluring. By staying busy, we get things done, amuse ourselves, and become successful. We obtain society's approval because it values active, fast-moving people. We gain a higher social status because industriousness is held in high esteem and idleness is not. In addition, we have a sense of power when we are busy. The mere movement of our hands gives us a feeling of being in control; the movement of our bodies produces a sense of well-being, sometimes of exhilaration. The "press of busyness is like a charm," wrote Kierkegaard. "It is sad to observe how its power swells, how it reaches out seeking always to lay hold of ever-younger victims so that childhood or youth are scarcely allowed the quiet and the retirement in which the Eternal may unfold a divine growth."[9]

Busyness is also attractive because it wards off being alone with ourselves. Being alone with ourselves in the presence of God can be a frightful prospect, for we might discover that what we think, say, and do is not worth thinking, saying, and doing. We might find that our lives do not have meaning and direction, or that deep within there is malice, pride, or self-deception. We might see that we love simply to obtain reward, that we want to succeed so that we can feed our egos, or that we have entered our vocation for no reason other than to justify our existence.

9. Kierkegaard, *Purity of Heart Is to Will One Thing*, p. 107.

Being busy with routine gives reassuring comfort. Creating a new life for ourselves can be fearful; we must give up old, familiar patterns and take risks with unexperienced ways of feeling and acting. By immersing ourselves in routine, we eliminate these risks. Busyness here acts as a tranquilizer, like a drug that soothes our fears and at the same time desensitizes us to life's great possibilities.

The busyness of active self-creation can also give us comfort, but of a different sort. We may not be afraid of newness or may not want to be passive spectators of life. We may have a strong distaste for falling into trivial routine and refuse to become victims of mindless conformity. So we plunge into activities — sensual ones, moral ones, religious ones even — to create a life of our own. In doing so, we prevent ourselves from succumbing to the dullness of routine, but we may be distracting ourselves nevertheless. Our self-creating activities might be motivated by the uneasy desire to run from the truth about ourselves. They might spring from the fear of what we will discover if solitude were to overtake us. When we engage in the busyness of active self-creation, it is as effective a tranquilizer as the busyness of routine.[10]

Busyness can also soothe away boredom, not just the "What shall I do now?" kind, but the nameless emptiness of whole-life boredom.[11] We feel weary and dissatisfied, not knowing what we want out of life. Everything seems hollow; we gaze at life with a vacant stare. What we need, we feel, is some new distraction — a project around the house, a visit from long-absent friends, an exciting movie — not recognizing that these do nothing to alter the meaninglessness behind the boredom.

In *A Life of One's Own,* Marion Milner describes how she once amassed activities to give herself a sense of purpose. "It seemed then," she writes, "that my purpose in life was to get the most out of life. And because I was not capable of more than very muddled thinking, I still assumed that the way to this was to strive to do more and more things; and this, in spite of my intuition about the need for

10. Becker, *The Denial of Death,* p. 84.
11. John Wild, *The Challenge of Existentialism* (Westport, Conn.: Greenwood Press, 1979), p. 36.

surrender."[12] Her striving, she says, was "a miser-like grabbing and piling up of experience." She was "always driving [herself] to do more things — to read more books, to learn more languages, to see more people, not to miss anything," all so that she could "get on" with things and be full of purpose.[13]

It is certainly possible to be attached to God while being active. Indeed, attachment to God incites certain kinds of activity. Busyness, however, diffuses that attachment. Our attention to him becomes sporadic and our single-minded love "slips more and more into oblivion."[14] God comes to feel like a dim memory. Our hold on the recognition that we need his forgiveness becomes precarious. Numbness creeps over us without our being aware that it is doing so.

One way, perhaps the only way, to counteract busyness is through silence — both empty, thoughtless silence and active, meditative silence in God's presence. What happens during periods of silence is that we empty our racing minds of their clutter and reorient our center of attention.[15] We let go of our need to "achieve and acquire."[16] As a result, our desire to justify our existence in self-enhancing ways dissipates. We do not feel pushed from within to compare ourselves with others or to use them to obtain rewards. We are freed from the fear of knowing our true motives and do not need to distract ourselves.

When we are silent, we can hear God more clearly. Our cares and worries do not muffle God's voice, as they so often do when we move hurriedly through our days. Our drive for self-aggrandizement does not obstruct God's gentle call to love self-forgetfully. Our impulse to conform does not screen out what God wishes for us to feel.

In times of silence, we find new directions for our lives and

12. Milner, *A Life of One's Own* (Los Angeles: J. P. Tarcher Publishing Co., 1981), p. 92.

13. Ibid., p. 90.

14. Kierkegaard, *Purity of Heart Is to Will One Thing*, p. 108.

15. "Solitude. . . . Its value lies in the greater possibility of attention" (Simone Weil, *Gravity and Grace*, trans. Arthur Wills [New York: Octagon Books, 1981], p. 175).

16. Irvin D. Yalom, *Existential Psychotherapy* (New York: Basic Books, 1980), p. 400.

meaning for what we do. Silence is a pause in life's headlong rush, a time when we ask ourselves where we are really going.

During some periods of silence, we discover painful truths about ourselves. We come to realize ways in which our hearts have gone astray, and we uncover areas of our lives from which we instinctively recoil. We find that we like in ourselves ulterior motives which we so dislike in others.

It is during times of silence like these that we experience God's grace most richly. We become overwhelmed by God's acceptance of us in spite of our continual yielding to motives that undermine single-minded love for him. The guilt we feel for yielding to these motives is displaced by gratitude for his loving us anyway.

It is important to note that silence is not by itself sufficient to counteract busyness. For we receive from silence what we put into it. If we put dark thoughts into silence, we are likely to end up in brooding depression. If all we want is time to nurse our worries, we will feel even more harassed. However, if we enter silence wanting to cast off distracting clutter, we will leave released and unharried.

Indifference

When we are indifferent toward something, it is of no importance to us. We are detached from it and have no curiosity about it. Our faces express no interest; we shrug our shoulders.

Pascal described indifference as "insensitivity to the greatest things," living "without a thought for the final end of life, drifting wherever [our] inclinations and pleasures may take [us]." Those who are indifferent do "not want to take the trouble" to investigate their eternal lot and feel "neither anxiety nor emotion" about losing everything through death. They are "unconcerned to seek the truth" and have no "desire that the eternal promises be true."[17]

Indifference is different from resistance. Resistance is active opposition, but indifference is having neither a special like nor a special

17. Pascal, "Against Indifference," *Pensées*, trans. A. J. Krailsheimer (New York: Penguin Books, 1966), pp. 156, 161, 158, 159.

dislike. When we resist doing something, we desire not to do it, but when we are indifferent toward it, we don't care one way or the other whether we do it. Indifference can, of course, come from resistance. We may say to ourselves, "No, I don't want to think about being open to God's grace." In putting the thought out of mind, we may forget about grace, and in time we may become unconcerned about it. Here the active resistance against grace produces lack of interest in it.

How can we tell what we really care about? How can we know that eternity matters to us?

We are not likely to be able to answer these questions with a simple inspection of our desires because the desires connected with these questions are not likely to be intuitively apparent to us. Although some desires are intuitively apparent, many are not. There are times when we wonder whether we genuinely love a prospective spouse, whether we feel the need to change jobs, or whether we want to do one thing on Saturday afternoon rather than another. Asking what we care about spiritually is often like wondering about these. We need to weigh want against want in order to find out.

One relatively straightforward method we can use to discover what matters to us is to notice the quantity of time taken up by various objects of our attention. The principle here is that what occupies our attention is an indicator of what we like. "Tell me where your attention lies and I will tell you who you are," wrote Ortega.[18] If our minds are occupied with ways we can impress others, then approval is what we most want. If our attention is absorbed by ways we can obtain more money, then money is what we most want. If our thoughts constantly turn to ways we can involve ourselves with persons of the opposite sex, then marriage or sex is what we most want. Falling in love is a perfect example of the principle: nearly every waking moment of the person who is in love is consumed with thoughts of the beloved.

Conversely, what is absent from our attention is an indication of what we are indifferent toward. If we rarely think about butterfly chasing, classical guitar music, or tennis, it is likely that we care little about them. And if the lover's attention becomes focused less and

18. Ortega y Gasset, *On Love: Aspects of a Single Theme,* trans. Toby Talbot (New York: New American Library–Meridian Books, 1957), p. 47.

less on the beloved, it is likely that she is falling out of love. This converse principle is not an infallible guide to indifference because we may unconsciously desire something to which we pay little conscious attention. And we may intensely desire something on some occasions even though we scarcely think about it on others. Apart from these kinds of cases, though, the principle is reliable: not thinking about ways we can give encouragement to acquaintances means that we probably are indifferent to doing so.

What, then, in general do we find occupying our consciousness? Perhaps the first feature we notice is the sheer quantity and variety of objects in it — images, desires, memories, impulses, feelings, anticipations, and inclinations. They shift and pulsate, often without our choosing, pulling us first in one direction and then in another. At any given moment, one or two dominate our consciousness, and during the course of an hour, many pass in and out of it.

A second feature is that some of these objects return to our consciousness more often than others. Those that do are the ones upon which our lives are focused. There are, perhaps, three or four such focuses, and there may be one which returns to our consciousness so often that it has become the chief focus of our lives.

Thus, if a sense of eternity does not occupy any of our attention, we probably are entirely indifferent to it. And if it does not return to our consciousness much, it is not likely to be one of the three or four focuses of our lives. The multitude of other objects have crowded it out. However, if a sense of eternity does occupy our attention, it matters to us, and if it occupies a great deal of our attention, it matters to us a great deal.

Attention is not only an indicator of what matters to us; it can also be a creator of it. If we spend time attending to God, love for him may follow.[19] This is not true of everyday objects, such as pencils, flowerpots, lawns, and rivers. Simply attending to these is not likely to bring about love for them. It is different with God, though, because he made us originally with a disposition to love

---

19. "If we turn our mind toward the good, it is impossible that little by little the whole soul will not be attracted thereto in spite of itself" (Simone Weil, *Gravity and Grace,* p. 170).

him. This disposition is blunted by self-centeredness, but it is awakened by attention. We are drawn to God when we focus our minds on his love for us; our indifference is punctured when we direct our awareness to his grace.

Directing our attention to God is not the only creator of love for him, nor is it always sufficient to awaken love. Melting of resistance may also be necessary and so also may the experience of being loved. When these are present, however, directing our attention to God attracts us to him almost irresistibly.

Attentiveness, the opposite of indifference, exhibits itself in various ways. I want to mention three: spiritual fervor, delight, and a sense of adventure.

Spiritual fervor is being absorbed in giving away love, yearning for an uncluttered heart, pondering the point of our lives, caring not for trivial pursuits. It is alertness to others' inner pain, willingness to be interrupted, troubling ourselves with others' needs. It is an irresistible attraction to eternity, an infinite interest, a passionate love, and a "willingness to follow every least hint from God."[20] Sometimes it is boundless enthusiasm and warm exuberance. More often it is quiet intensity, patient vitality, and tranquil and undisturbed directedness.

Delight exhibits itself never more keenly than when children open gifts. They bubble over with intense anticipation, spontaneous wonder, excited glee, unbounded exhilaration, the impulse to skip and twirl with carefree abandon, and the feeling that someone likes them. We would experience such delight if we thought of a friend as a gift, of God's grace as a gift, of contacts with people as gifts, or of having a little bit of eternity in our hearts as a gift. We too would anticipate opening them. Our days — and nights — would be marked by unrestrained felicity. We would dance with spontaneous merriment at having found the one thing for which we have longed.

Adventure involves newness, excitement, and spontaneity. With a sense of adventure, we become invigorated and acquire a freshness that renews the tired, mechanical pattern we sometimes find ourselves falling into. The spontaneity of adventure replaces the un-

---

20. Søren Kierkegaard, *The Sickness unto Death,* trans. Howard V. Hong and Edna H. Hong (Princeton: Princeton University Press, 1980), p. 103.

thinking "habit of piety" that can easily overtake us.[21] A spark flashes in us when we turn the duty of loving someone who is unlovable into an adventure.

Kierkegaard compared the spirited person to a lover. "A believer, after all, is a lover; as a matter of fact, when it comes to enthusiasm, the most rapturous lover of all lovers is but a stripling compared with a believer. Imagine a lover. Is it not true that he would be capable of speaking about his beloved all day long and all night, too, day in and day out?"[22] The lover constantly thinks about how she can please her beloved and conceives innumerable ways in which she can do so. Her creativity is boundless. She says, "Today I will write him a note, and tomorrow I will take his hand and squeeze it gently when he looks into my eyes. I won't say anything then, though, for my touch will convey all." And her look will be not rapturous, perhaps, but knowing, with a faint but revealing smile.

The believer, too, asks, "How can I love today? In what new ways can I sense eternity?"

It is important not to think of fervor, delight, and a sense of adventure as characteristics that we must possess whether we like them or not. We need instead to become the kind of persons that overflow with them.

Nor must we think that we should exhibit these throughout the day and half the night, despite the lover's propensity to do so. We must go through the pain and sorrow of contrition, the drudgery of everyday duties, and the detachment required by analytical thinking. We need large amounts of evenhanded calm and quietness. The pursuit of eternity does not come just from enthusiasm. All it needs is a momentary burst of delight one month, a spark of adventure another, a flash of consuming passion the third, and in between, strenuous and often painful work.

21. "God might forgive cowardice and passion, but was it possible to forgive the habit of piety? . . . . Salvation could strike like lightning at the evil heart, but the habit of piety excluded everything but the evening prayer and the Guild meeting and the feel of humble lips on your gloved hand" (Graham Greene, *The Power and the Glory* [New York: Bantam Books, 1968], p. 161).

22. Kierkegaard, *The Sickness unto Death*, p. 82.

Sometimes the work required is so demanding that we become weary of it. We lose our freshness and vigor; our endurance wanes; we become fatigued and worn out. Eventually indifference overtakes us, and we no longer care about love.

Although indifference comes from weariness, the two are not the same. Indifference can exist before we work, whereas weariness occurs only after we work. Indifference — sloth — is one of the seven deadly sins, but weariness is a natural result of effort. We become tired of giving ourselves to others, of praying, of taking goodness seriously, of being a Christian.

Sometimes weariness becomes life threatening. We feel that we cannot go on; we are burned out by living. This is an ultimate weariness that makes us feel too tired to continue. What can we do when we are hit by this kind of tiredness?

One thing we can do is to go through the motions even though we don't feel like it. We can make ourselves act compassionately even though we would rather be at home lying on the couch. We can open our Bibles and read even though we really want to be watching television. Sometimes the weariness goes away by itself. We must not suppose that inner motivation always precedes action; sometimes it is the reverse. However, when our weariness does not go away when we use this strategy, simply going through the motions becomes an intolerable emptiness. What can we do then?

We can take a rest, go on an inner retreat, and be silent. We can remove ourselves from the demands of life for a time — a few minutes, an hour, an afternoon, or longer — and listen to God.

We can eliminate inessential activities and reduce the amount of energy we expend on essential ones — work, home maintenance, transportation. If these wear us out, we will have little vigor for anything else. The same is true for Christian activities. If we are overloaded with them, we will soon want to give them all up.

We can also reduce the amount of energy we expend on helping others and giving them sacrificial love. Although we need to hear again and again that the "fat relentless ego" is a chief obstacle to a Christlike life and that loving self-forgetfully is our Christian vocation, we also need to hear that too much giving and not enough receiving can shut us down.[23] We cannot, in fact, give without first receiving. We cannot take care of others without first taking care of ourselves. So to restore ourselves when weariness strikes, we can put others' needs aside for a while and tend to our own needs.

In addition, we can associate with people who will give us support and let their caring soak in. Often, indeed, we can scarcely continue without such caring. Though we fear that they will interpret our needing them as a sign of weakness, it is really a sign of maturity to admit that we cannot easily live the Christian life alone.

Finally, we can bring ourselves to accept and feel deeply God's healing love. Doing so will give us a sense of stability during times of deepest weariness.

Resistance

Counselors, therapists, and psychiatrists discover very soon that their counselees, though they want to be healed, also resist being healed.[24] Gentle questioning about sensitive matters produces both honest and evasive responses. Too much probing at the wrong time or in the wrong way brings resistance and sometimes anger. What the counselor must do is learn how to lead the counselee into painful memories and feelings without triggering defense mechanisms. •

A Christian's spiritual life is marked by a similar ambivalence. Ideas from a sermon, a book, or a friend produce both contrition and evasion. Thoughts about forgiveness that pop into one's mind bring acceptance and defensiveness. Like the counselee, the Christian both seeks and resists knowing her true feelings about self-justification. In what follows I shall explore the resistance side of this ambivalence.

23. The phrase "fat relentless ego" comes from Iris Murdoch: "In the moral life the enemy is the fat relentless ego." (See "On 'God' and 'Good,'" in *Revisions: Changing Perspectives in Moral Philosophy,* ed. Stanley Hauerwas and Alasdair MacIntyre [Notre Dame: University of Notre Dame Press, 1983], p. 72.)

24. "The patient wants to be cured — but he also wants not to be" (Sigmund Freud, *The Question of Lay Analysis,* ed. and trans. James Strachey [New York: W. W. Norton, 1959], p. 57).

Perhaps the first thing to say about resistance is that we resist singleness of heart itself for several reasons. The first is that singleness of heart is too big and too intense. When we think about everything it entails, we draw back from it with the feeling that it is more than we can possess. With singleness of heart we love for the sake of love, not for its reward. We live as individuals who do not lose their identity in others; we set aside self-justification and allow grace to permeate us. We think creatively and passionately about loving, not retreating into our imaginations and not letting busyness distract us. We feel warm delight, overflowing gratitude, and imperturbable peace.

There is a largeness here that we cannot take in. The feeling is somewhat like the awe we experience when we first view a magnificent panorama of mountains, or see the Grand Canyon or Niagara Falls for the first time, or observe miles of billowy clouds from an airplane, or stare at the stars on a cloudless night. We cannot keep looking without being overcome by the magnitude of what we see. We feel that we must shut down or focus on a single part to keep ourselves from exploding.

Ernest Becker calls this resistance a "refusal of reality." We hold the world at bay, he says, keeping our minds on small segments of it. We "partialize" the world and narrow it down so that we do not have to face its expansiveness. It is not just death that makes us tremble, Becker says, but life.[25]

We are, to be sure, drawn to the magnificent panorama, but when we get there, we do little more than glance at it. We are also attracted to the something more that Christ offers ("I came that they may have life, and have it abundantly" [John 10:10]), but when it is presented to us, we take very little of it. It is as if we want to be constricted, preferring a living death to life's lavishness.

The second reason we resist singleness of heart is that we like doing the things that undermine it. We like being admired for our Christian virtues. We like congratulating ourselves, justifying ourselves, and making comparisons. We like retreating into imagination and burying ourselves in activities. Though we also want not to do

25. Becker, *The Denial of Death*, p. 178.

these things and feel remorse when we discover that we have, we like doing them nevertheless.

The intensity with which we like doing things that undermine singleness of heart reveals the strength of our resistance to it. We enjoy immensely the expansive feeling that self-admiration brings. We would rather give up our dearest possessions than cease justifying ourselves. We must, then, in spite of our earnest quest for singleness, resist it with a good deal of energy.[26]

This fact is reinforced by the third reason we resist singleness of heart — apprehension about the newness it brings. The lifelong habits, the desires and thinking patterns to which we have become accustomed — all feel right. They are like old friends. We are comfortable with them, and when we have to part from them, we feel uneasy. Though we are attracted to simplicity of heart, we cling to the familiar ways of wanting and acting because they give us security. We have lived with self-congratulation and self-justification for so long and so lovingly that leaving them feels like leaving home.

Augustine pinpoints this source of resistance in his account of his conversion: "The nearer came that moment in time when I was to become something different, the greater terror did it strike into me." He continues, "My lovers of old, trifles of trifles and vanities of vanities, held me back. They plucked at my fleshly garment, and they whispered softly: 'Do you cast us off?' and 'From that moment we shall no more be with you forever and ever!'"[27]

In addition to resisting singleness of heart directly, we resist it indirectly by not wanting to know the motives and barriers that undermine it. We do not want to know that we use our Christian virtues for self-justification, that we congratulate ourselves for belonging to a certain kind of church, or compare our qualities to those of others. We evade knowing that our love is more imaginary than real and that secretly we want recognition for the real love we

26. "If God is to save our souls, he must do so with people who for the most part fight tooth and nail against the process" (Frederick Buechner, in the foreword to Jill P. Baumgaertner's *Flannery O'Connor: A Proper Scaring* [Wheaton, Ill.: Harold Shaw Publishers, 1988], p. ix).

27. Augustine, *Confessions,* trans. John K. Ryan (Garden City, N.Y.: Doubleday–Image Books, 1960), Book 8, Chapter 11, p. 200.

do have. We deny that we think of our identities as being based on possessions, job performance, and social status. We especially evade knowing that we like the motives and barriers that undermine single-ness of heart, and even more so evade knowing that we evade.

·The situation is like that when we remember dreams in which we have killed someone who has hurt us or have acted sexually with someone with whom it is forbidden to do so. The memory of the dream pops into consciousness later in the day. For an instant, perhaps, we relish the thought of the killing or the sex. But just as instantaneously we become horrified that we have dreamed of it and push the dream out of mind (though not so quickly that we do not get a little more pleasure from it). We do not want to know that we have had the dream or that we have liked it. We also do not want to know that we do not want to know these things.

Pascal observed that this resistance to self-knowledge exhibits itself in what he called "diversion." Diversion occurs, he said, when we take our minds off ourselves because we are unable to bear what we will find when we look inside. There are two "secret instincts" within us. One is "left over from the greatness of our original nature, telling us that the only true happiness lies in rest and not in excite-ment." The other drives us to "seek external diversion and occupa-tion." It makes us restless and causes us to avert our gaze from inner chaos. Because of this instinct, we feel happy only if we are "diverted from thinking of what we are, either by some occupation which takes our mind off it or by some novel and agreeable passion which keeps us busy."[28]

In the *Pensées* Pascal describes a number of ways in which we engage in diversion. Ordinary activity is one. We shun rest; we "would do anything to be disturbed." We are "fond of hustle and bustle"; the pleasures of solitude are incomprehensible to us. Another is "the hunt." Hunters would not be satisfied if they were presented with a deer or a pheasant, which shows, Pascal says, that they prefer the hunt to the capture. We are like hunters. What we want is not "the easy and peaceful life that allows us to think of our unhappy condition . . . , but

28. Pascal, "Diversion," *Pensées*, trans. A. J. Krailsheimer (Baltimore: Penguin Books, 1966), pp. 67-69.

the agitation that takes our mind off it and diverts us." Still another method of diversion is being preoccupied with cares and worries. If these were taken away, we "would see ourselves and think about what we are, where we come from, and where we are going."[29]

There are other ways we resist knowing what goes on inside us. When we read the Bible or a devotional book, listen to a talk, or sit in a church service, we might do so merely with the aim of discovering spiritual truths about humankind instead of with the aim of uncovering our own hidden drives. The excited "Aha!" of mental recognition makes us think we have probed our own interiors. What it really does is distance us from ourselves. We do not notice that in wanting to know about humanity in general, even in passionately wanting to have this knowledge, our real intention is to run from ourselves. And though we would disavow this impersonalist evasion, though we hear countless times that we must believe with our hearts and not just with our minds, we succumb to it nevertheless. It is an effective way of convincing ourselves that we do believe with our hearts and at the same time evading believing with our hearts.

Another way of resisting self-knowledge is "the other-person maneuver." This occurs when we focus attention on others in order to deflect attention from ourselves. It can happen when we are much concerned about the sins of other Christians, their lifelessness and inconsistencies, but are without a proportionate concern for our own need to receive mercy.[30] It can happen in the opposite way too: we can take such active and solicitous interest in others' welfare that we do not notice that we have an inner life that needs attending to. It can also happen when we attribute the unpleasant truths we discover about human nature to other people. Here we attribute the truths not to specific individuals but to "them." The "them" is not humanity in general, as in the impersonalist evasion; it is a group — those who

29. Pascal, "Diversion," p. 68.

30. "And furthermore, 'tis a sign that affections are not of the right sort, if persons seem to be much affected with the bad qualities of their fellow Christians, as the coldness and lifelessness of other saints, but are in no proportion affected with their own defects and corruptions" (Jonathan Edwards, *Treatise on Religious Affections* [New Haven: Yale University Press, 1959], p. 370).

are different from us or those who are not Christians. "We" are exempt from the unpleasant truths we discover, but "they" are not.

The other-person maneuver is a way of engaging in straightforward denial. We think defensively, "That's not true of me," because we dislike discovering ulterior motives in ourselves. Our immediate reaction to the thought that we congratulate ourselves is to think, "I don't do that." On occasion this denial occurs even when we clearly see what we are doing. In Dostoyevsky's *Crime and Punishment*, Raskalnikov, while sewing a sling in his coat to hold the fatal ax, while carefully wrapping the fake package with which he intended to deceive the old pawnbroker, and while stealthily stealing the ax from the janitor's room, "could not in all this time believe for one minute in the carrying out of his plan."[31] We refuse to believe that we are striving for success to justify ourselves because we see that doing so conflicts with the grace we have experienced or think we have experienced.

Both the impersonalist evasion and the other-person maneuver can be directed inward. We might avidly search for self-knowledge in an impersonal way, thinking of ourselves as an object of curiosity in which we have purely objective interest. Or we might treat ourselves as an other, disassociating ourselves from our own self-congratulation and pursuit of reward.[32] Each of these ways of resisting self-knowledge gives the illusion of seeking self-knowledge.

Identification with an ideal blocks self-knowledge in the same way that denial does. When we read about Christian virtues, we say to ourselves, "Yes, those are what characterize me." Though we do not normally actually whisper this to ourselves or formulate the sentence in our minds, we do have the thought half-consciously, experiencing it as a warm glow or a calm satisfaction with ourselves. Our impulse to believe that we are heroes — Christian heroes — is

31. Dostoyevsky, *Crime and Punishment*, trans. Sidney Monas (New York: New American Library, 1968), p. 76.

32. "We find it very hard to identify our sin with our own will and our own malice. On the contrary, we naturally tend to interpret our immoral act as an involuntary mistake, or as the malice of a spirit in us that is other than ourself" (Thomas Merton, *New Seeds of Contemplation* [1961; rpt. New York: New Directions, 1972], p. 113).

so strong that we identify with attractive qualities almost instinctively. Of course, we may really possess these qualities. But the instinct to identify with them is not what tells us this.

"Copying" other people's beliefs blocks self-knowledge too. Kierkegaard once wrote in his journal, "There are many people who arrive at the result of their lives like schoolboys; they cheat their teacher by copying the answer from the key in the arithmetic book, without bothering to do the sum for themselves."[33] We copy others' beliefs when we live outside ourselves, unconsciously adopting the beliefs of those with whom we identify. This can happen while we are listening to a minister or reading a book. We copy what we hear or read so that the beliefs we come to have are really someone else's.

We are vulnerable to copying in a variety of contexts. If we are part of a rigid, authoritarian church, we may copy to avoid others' disapproval. If we are part of a loving, accepting church, we may copy to imagine ourselves being loving and accepting. In either case our being an external person is an obstacle to knowing what goes on inside us.

Not all copying, it should be noted, interferes with self-knowledge. Consciously imitating someone's virtues does not. Such imitating can in fact incite us to peer inward. It is unconscious copying that makes us think we are something we are not.

This sketch of ways we resist knowing ourselves suggests that resisting self-knowledge pervades nearly everything we do. Pascal was on target when he noted that "all our life passes in this way."[34] Resistance is not an isolated feature of human existence.

What do we get from resistance? We get more self-congratulation, self-justification, and reward, plus an enhanced sense of self-worth. We perpetuate the secret delights of imagination and the gratification that busyness produces. We remain in blissful ignorance of unpalatable desires.

This ignorance, we now see, is not like everyday ignorance, because it is self-induced. We deliberately forget our moments of

33. Kierkegaard, *The Diary of Søren Kierkegaard,* ed. Peter Rohde (New York: Carol Publishing Group, 1960), p. 14.
34. Pascal, "Diversion," p. 69.

self-admiration and consciously overlook the exaggerated sense of self-worth that drives us. We genuinely do not know what motivates us, but it is by choice that this is so. Kierkegaard describes the subtle way in which this willful ignorance develops. We seldom deliberately do what is wrong, he says, knowing at the time that it is wrong. Rather, "willing allows some time to elapse, an interim called: 'We shall look at it tomorrow.' During . . . this, knowing becomes more and more obscure, and the lower nature gains the upper hand more and more."[35] Gradually the awareness of our reward-seeking and self-justifying becomes clouded until finally it is eclipsed altogether. We have convinced ourselves that we are single-minded recipients of God's grace.

35. Kierkegaard, *The Sickness unto Death*, p. 94.

Chapter 5

Illusory Experiences of Grace

With the allurements of sweet odors I am not much troubled: when they are absent, I do not seek them, and when they are present, I do not reject them, but I am prepared to do entirely without them. So do I seem to myself, but perhaps I am deceived. Within me are those lamentable dark areas wherein my own capacities lie hidden from me. Hence, when my mind questions itself about its own powers, it is not easy for it to decide what should be believed. For even what is within it is for the most part hidden away unless brought to light by some experience. In this life, the whole of which is termed a trial, no one should be sure whether one who can pass from worse to better might not also pass from being better to worse. One hope, one trust, one firm promise — your mercy.

Augustine, *Confessions*

From time to time I have described how a given motive may cause us to develop an illusion. Our fear of disapproval, for example, may make us think we are Christians even though we are not. The fear not only makes us act in Christian ways so that other people think we are Christians, but it makes us experience certain feelings so that we ourselves become convinced we are Christians.

I want now to discuss illusions regarding the experience that traditional Christianity says is central to being a Christian — openness to God's grace. I shall show that illusory experiences of grace do indeed exist and shall explain how we come to have them.

Before doing so, however, I want to point out that I am using "experience" broadly to include decisive encounters in emotional contexts, calm convictions in tranquil settings, and enduring attitudes. Grace is experienced in different ways, and my claim that illusions occur applies to all of these ways. I am not targeting one of them to the exclusion of the others, for encounters, convictions, and attitudes are equally susceptible to illusion.

The two key facts about illusion that concern me here are, first, that in an illusion what appears to us does not really exist, and second, that we do not know that we are mistaken about the appearance. This second fact does not characterize every illusion. We know that railroad tracks do not converge in the distance and that sticks in water are not bent even though the tracks appear to converge and the sticks appear to be bent. Illusory experiences of grace are not like these natural illusions. When we experience grace in an illusory way, we do not know that the experience does not correspond to anything in reality. We mistakenly believe that we are open to God's forgiving love and are unaware of this mistake at the time we have the belief.

"But," we should ask, "how can we be mistaken about being open to grace? It is a state with which we are directly acquainted, like having a headache or being warm. Can we think we have a headache even though we do not or think we are warm when we are cold? There is nothing about these experiences that could make them illusory. When we know we are guilty before God, confess that guilt to him, and receive his freely given forgiveness, we can be sure that we have experienced God's grace. Such experiences are not the kind of thing about which we can be mistaken because we know them immediately and directly.

"Moreover," we should also ask, "does not the Bible tell us that we can know what our status with God is? John writes, 'I write these things to you . . . so that you may know that you have eternal life' (1 John 5:13). What would be the point of the Bible's describing redemption from sin if we could not know we possess it? Numerous passages declare God's love for us, and they would be charades if we were subject to illusion regarding it."

When we think about these questions, I believe we should have a blend of confidence and distrust. Although the Bible states that we can know we are open to God's grace, it also recommends an attentive self-examination on the grounds that we may be mistaken. Put conversely, we are enjoined by Jesus and the Old Testament prophets to be skeptical about our faith, but we are also given assurance about faith. I shall deal with the confidence we may have in the next chapter; here I shall explain why that confidence should be tempered by distrust.

First, notice that we are sometimes mistaken about everyday feelings. We might accept an invitation to visit with friends, at first thinking we will enjoy being with them. Later reflection reveals, however, that we accepted the invitation simply to please our friends, not because we wanted to be with them. Or imagine that we are hiking in a forest and the trail we are on comes dangerously close to a deep ravine. We walk on, at first with physical movements and feelings of apparent unconcern, but as we continue we realize that our first reaction really covered up fear. Or suppose that lately we have easily become angry with a friend or a spouse. At first we do not know why we have been feeling the way we have, but then we discover, with the aid of a book or therapist, that long pent-up anger toward a parent has surfaced.

In each of these situations, we are mistaken about a feeling — in the first two, about what the feeling is, and in the third, about the object of the feeling. It is not that we did not know what we felt and later clarified our inner state, though this situation does sometimes occur. Nor is it that we first felt one thing and later felt another, though this too sometimes occurs. Rather, we thought we felt one thing or thought the object of our feeling was one thing, when in fact it was quite different. So although we cannot be mistaken about some feelings, such as physical warmth, we can about others.

The second step in showing that we can have illusory experiences of grace is to show that we can be mistaken not just about certain everyday feelings, but about moral and religious feelings as well. We may be tempted not to report all of our income on our income tax return, but we do so anyway, feeling what we take to be a strong sense of duty. Later, when we think about the situation, the picture of a disapproving parent flashes into our mind, and we become aware that it was not duty we felt but desire to please that parent. This example shows that we can really be feeling fear of disapproval when we think we are feeling duty. The two have the same strong "push" and can be confused with one another in certain circumstances.

We may believe we have inner peace — the "peace of God, which surpasses all understanding" (Phil. 4:7) — but when we probe a bit, we discover uneasiness about how well we are living the Christian life or restlessness at our inability to let God love us. We find envy of those who are more well-liked than we are or a vague sense of having wasted our lives. Our belief that we are free from these feelings may come from our belief that Christians are supposed to possess inner peace. Or we may mistake harmonious relations with others for inner harmony, or so identify with someone who appears to have inner peace that we imagine we have it as well.

So, again, we can be mistaken about what we feel, this time about more significant emotions. If this is so, it is not surprising to discover that we can also be mistaken about experiences that bear on our relation to God. We should not let our desperate desire to have this relation settled cloud the realization that our beliefs can be illusive. Indeed, the book that most vividly depicts the urgency of securing a right relation to God also calls for skepticism and distrust.

One of the most striking pictures in the Bible is the scene of the Last Judgment in Matthew 25. The image portrayed there is one in which a huge throng of people is gathered around a throne on which Jesus is seated. He is going to separate the people into two groups, and the criterion he is going to use to determine which people go into which group is whether or not they have fed him, given him something to drink, or visited him when he was sick or in prison. He makes the separation, placing those who pass the test on his right and those who fail on his left. People in each group are surprised that Jesus has put them where they are because they do not know when they did or did not come to his aid. They ask, "When did we see you hungry, thirsty, sick or in prison?" and Jesus answers, "If you fed or visited someone whom you knew was hungry or sick,

80

it was as if you fed or visited me, and if you did not feed or visit someone whom you knew was hungry or sick, it was as if you did not feed or visit me."

This picture of the Last Judgment contains an explicit indication that we might be wrong about which group we think we will end up in. Of course, part of the point of Jesus' narrative is to stir us to embrace the humble compassion that is characteristic of those who associate with people at the bottom level of society, which is where the hungry usually are. These same elements — the possibility of error and the urging to transformation — are vividly displayed in the story of the Pharisee and the tax collector in Luke 18.

Although we are not told in the story that the Pharisee believed himself to be right with God, his manner of speaking shows that he did believe this. Yet the tax collector went home in the right and not the Pharisee. Jesus' use of the word "justified" to characterize the tax collector shows that the story is not just about an everyday virtue. We have here a picture of a good religious person who mistakenly thought his position with God was assured.

Our first reaction to this picture is to agree: "Yes, there is a religious hypocrite." And perhaps we secretly add, "I'm glad I'm not like him." The reaction Jesus wanted us to have, however, is distrust of our own beliefs about our relation to God. We are informed that the parable was told "to some who trusted in themselves that they were righteous" (v. 9). To realize that we are more like the Pharisee than we have thought (without using this realization to feel superior to those who do not realize it) is to experience the self-suspicion the story is meant to incite.

The Old Testament prophets, too, provoke distrust in the genuineness of our God-experiences. The prophets denounced not just the idol worship and the child sacrifice of heathens, and not just intrusions into the Israelites' worship from pagan religions, but also the false religiosity of the Israelites. This false religiosity consisted of traditional practices done without feeling. David captured the thought in his confessional psalm: "For you have no delight in sacrifice; if I were to give a burnt offering, you would not be pleased. The sacrifice acceptable to God is a broken spirit; a broken and contrite heart, O God, you will not despise" (Ps. 51:16-17). The persons the prophets had in mind in describing false religiosity were the ones who participated in the prescribed sacrifices, thinking that they were thereby satisfying God. Perhaps David himself was in this situation after he took Bathsheba and had her husband killed to avoid embarrassment over the resulting pregnancy. Nathan's ringing "You are the man!" brought him out of his illusion (2 Sam. 11–12).

In addition to moral and religious urgency, then, and in addition to love, joy, peace, patience, and kindness, the Bible enjoins skepticism. This skepticism is not about other people's experiences with God, and it is not skepticism in general — an abstract attitude that distances us from our own experiences. It is skepticism turned inward. It is asking ourselves whether we have arrived at what we think is a state of grace by some illusion-producing mechanism. It is probing our feelings to see whether the desire for self-justification, the fear of disapproval, or self-congratulation has caused us to think that we are open to grace.

The last step in showing that experiences of grace can be illusory is to describe how such illusions happen and what brings them about. Consider two of the examples I have already mentioned. In the case of the social invitation, we had the idea that we wanted to be with our friends, but that did not represent anything because we really had no desire to be with them. We thought we had the desire because we focused our attention on the idea and mistook it for the desire. Similarly, in the case of thinking we felt inner peace, we had the idea of what that peace is like, but again we wrongly identified the idea of peace with the peace itself. It is the same with an illusory experience of grace. We have the idea of grace, and we mistake the idea for the reality.

"But," we should ask, "how can anyone think that an idea of something is the thing itself? The two are so unlike each other that it is hard to imagine their being confused, especially when they involve intense inner states such as contrition."

The answer is that confusing the two is common even though they are unlike each other and even though we know they are unlike each other. The case in which a woman loves a man solely for his wealth illustrates this singular fact. She conceives herself as loving him without ulterior motives. The idea she has of her love for him is very pleasant to her, and perhaps she becomes enthralled with it on occasion. If she knew that her real attraction to him is his wealth, she would see that her idea of loving him does not represent any real love. As it is, she does not know what her real attraction is, so she imagines she loves him. If we were to present her with the difference between the idea of love and real love, she would respond that of course she knows the difference and protest that she has real love. Her unconscious attraction blinds her to the fact that she has fallen in love merely with the idea of love.

Such a state can also occur with other unconscious motives. We might think of ourselves as being compassionate when in reality we are motivated by fear of disapproval. We may believe we love God even though unconscious identification with others' love of God causes that belief. In each case we have an idea that we mistake for the reality. We know the difference between the two, but the fear of disapproval and the unconscious identification conceal our attraction to the ideas.

The presence of these unconscious motives means that knowledge of our own internal states is not as immediate and direct as we might suppose. The desire for reward, self-congratulation, and self-justification intervene and distort in roughly the same way that a thick fog hinders our perception of distant physical objects. The motives undermining singleness of heart operate in us to produce not only ambivalence but illusion as well. Sometimes the motives battle genuine acceptance of God's forgiveness, and sometimes they make us think we have such acceptance when in fact we do not.

Illusory experiences of grace arise in a number of ways. When self-congratulation is intense, we might mistakenly think we have God's love in us. Thomas Merton describes how this can happen:

> The pleasure that is in his heart when he does difficult things and succeeds in doing them well, tells him secretly: "I am a saint." . . . The pleasure burns into a devouring fire. The warmth of that fire feels very much like the love of God. . . . He burns with self-admiration and thinks: "It is the fire of the love of God."
> He thinks his own pride is the Holy Ghost.[1]

1. Merton, *New Seeds of Contemplation* (1961; rpt. New York: New Directions, 1972), pp. 49-50.

Comparing ourselves with others can give us an exalted sense of importance that we may mistake for God's accepting us. Because we often imagine our status with God to be what it is with people, we conceive ourselves to be acceptable to God when we conceive ourselves acceptable to people because of our imagined superiority. The self-directedness of comparison is an indication that we are victims of illusion. If we constantly think we are "eminent saint[s], much distinguished in Christian experience," it is likely that we are not.[2]

We may have learned to use Christian language perfectly in order to fit into a church, but mistake the ability to talk Christianity with the real thing. We "hear but do not have any concrete experience or correlated understanding of the meaning of the language of grace. The words of grace as they resound in Scripture and the liturgy, in the creed and in doctrine, may be passively received and assented to, but have little relation whatever to [our] religious experience."[3]

We may imagine ourselves to be the recipients of grace in the same illusory way we imagine ourselves to be better looking or more popular than we really are. We may confuse approval of other Christians with God's approval of us. We may unwittingly substitute acceptance of statements about Christ for acceptance of Christ himself.

We might refrain from acting in certain ways to get the esteem of fellow Christians and think of this refraining as conversion. We might identify desire for moral or social improvement with contrition. We might even believe mere inclusion in a church makes us acceptable to God. Or we may think that vigorous defense of Christian beliefs justifies us.[4]

We may think of God's forgiveness as a general truth ("Everyone needs God's forgiveness") and substitute the belief in this general truth for personal acceptance. We may imagine that we are open to

2. Jonathan Edwards, *Treatise on Religious Affections* (New Haven: Yale University Press, 1959), p. 329.

3. Roger Haight, *The Experience and Language of Grace* (Ramsey, N.J.: Paulist Press, 1979), pp. 12-13.

4. "Some *strong* defenders of the faith are expressing their unconscious hostility through their caustic verbal assaults on those who do not share their beliefs. They act in the name of Christianity, but out of unconscious angry feelings" (James Dolby, *I, Too, Am Man* [Waco, Tex.: Word Books, 1969], p. 30).

God's grace simply because others are. We may take a certain kind of emotional excitement to be acceptance of God's love. We may possess sorrow only as an "official feeling," one that we adopt because we are supposed to and not because we want to. We might delight in being virtuous and think thereby that we are delighting in grace.

Jonathan Edwards describes how he was once a victim of this last illusion:

> When I was a boy, some years before I went to college . . . , I experienced I know not what kind of delight in religion. My mind was much engaged in it, and had much self-righteous pleasure; and it was my delight to abound in religious duties. I with some of my schoolmates joined together, and built a booth in a swamp, in a very retired spot, for a place of prayer. And besides, I had particular secret places of my own in the woods, where I used to retire by myself; and was from time to time much affected. My affections seemed to be lively and easily moved, and I seemed to be in my element when engaged in religious duties. And I am ready to think, many are deceived with such affections, and such a kind of delight as I then had in religion, and mistake it for grace.[5]

"But," we should ask again, "are these cases really illusions? Does not the mistake in them consist of adopting a 'works' approach to God, as Paul puts it in Ephesians 2:8-9, instead of a grace approach? People in these cases think they are acceptable to God because of some merit they possess, such as superiority to other Christians, and not because of God's free gift. So although the cases illustrate mistaken ways of making ourselves acceptable to God, they do not illustrate illusion."

This question requires us to distinguish between two kinds of illusion. When we take a works approach to God, we mistakenly think we are acceptable to God because of our works. When we have an illusory experience of grace, we mistakenly think we are acceptable to God because of what we wrongly take to be an expe-

---

5. Edwards, "Personal Narrative," in *Voices from the Heart: Four Centuries of American Piety,* ed. Roger Lundin and Mark A. Noll (Grand Rapids: Wm. B. Eerdmans, 1987), pp. 70-71.

rience of God's grace. If we think we are acceptable to God solely because of our superiority, we are under the first kind of illusion. But if our superiority makes us think we have experienced God's grace when in fact we have not, we possess the second kind.

The motives undermining singleness of heart can produce both kinds of illusion. Self-admiration, for example, can cause us to feel acceptable to God by making us feel that we are decent and admirable persons who are worthy of God's respect. Self-admiration can also make us think that God has given us grace, for we can mistake the self-admiration for the experience of being given grace.

From one perspective the difference between these two kinds of illusion does not matter much. Both can be just as subtle and difficult to detect. Although we know that church attendance does not make us acceptable to God, we may unconsciously use it in this way. We may also use it in this way even though we are fluent in the language of grace and imagine (without suspecting we are doing so) that we have experienced grace. Waking up from one kind of illusion can be just as startling as waking up from the other.

As little as we want to admit it, then, we must conclude that our religious experiences can be illusory. The consequences of this conclusion are significant. First, because other people are a source of our illusion, as we saw earlier, and because for us these other people are Christians if we ourselves are Christians, we have to infer that the Christian church is a source of our illusion. Also, since we are part of the church, we are as much a source of other Christians' illusion as they are a source of ours. Although the Christian church is a repository of truth about the human condition and about the way God deals with that condition, it is also the origin of illusion regarding these. In it "people are effectively defended and shielded against immediate religious experience."[6]

Moreover, if we are victims of illusion, we do not know who we really are and what drives us.[7] If comparison unconsciously

6. C. G. Jung, *Psychology and Religion,* vol. 2 of *The Collected Works of C. G. Jung* (Princeton: Princeton University Press, 1969), p. 43..

7. "We are not very good at recognizing illusions, least of all the ones we cherish about ourselves" (Thomas Merton, *New Seeds of Contemplation,* p. 34).

moves us to exhibit love and humility, we possess a fundamental misconception about ourselves. If self-congratulation unknowingly incites us to act as model Christians, then again our real selves are hidden from us.

In addition, our standing with God may be different from what we think it is. Since being open to grace determines our standing with God, and since we can be mistaken about whether we are open to grace, we can be mistaken about our standing with God. This consequence can be rather unsettling, especially if we have been comfortably assuming for years that we have been open to grace, and suddenly become aware of hidden motives that have made us closed to that grace.

It follows from these consequences that illusion is more deadly to faith than overt opposition. Overt opposition is open and evident, but illusion sneaks up on us and ensnares us without our knowledge. The real challenge of faith involves rooting out self-congratulation and self-justification, eliminating comparisons, removing the impulse to live outside ourselves, and getting rid of attraction to reward and fear of disapproval. Meeting this challenge is "the moral equivalent of war."[8]

8. William James, "The Moral Equivalent of War," in *The Writings of William James* (New York: Modern Library, 1968), pp. 660-71.

Chapter 6

Openness to Grace

> *The mercy of God . . . can be the most painful thing in our lives to learn to live with, respond to, bear. "My yoke is easy, and my burden is light" — but only to the degree that we cast off the burden of ego with which we are heavily laden, in order to be yoked and balmed by this fiery, purifying mercy.*
>
> Maggie Ross, *The Fire of Your Life*

We have looked at motives that undermine singleness of heart, and we have seen not only that they pull us away from grace but that they can make us think we have it when in fact we do not. They contribute both to ambivalence and to illusion. We must now ask how we can detect what Jonathan Edwards has called "false appearances of grace."[1] What can we do to determine that what we think is openness to grace really is?

The answer I shall give is threefold. We can compare our experiences of grace both with what we know such experiences are not and with what we know such experiences are. We can also compare the effects of our experiences with what we know are the effects of being open to grace.

1. Edwards, *Treatise on Religious Affections* (New Haven: Yale University Press, 1959), p. 86.

My aim in giving this answer is to give a foundation for the confidence that I believe should go hand in hand with the distrust we should have toward experiences of grace. Although the presence of hidden motives should make us distrust our claims to have experienced grace, we can balance this distrust with well-founded assurance. By using the three tests I shall describe, we can come to know that we have experienced grace.

The two elements of openness to grace I shall focus on are contrition and acceptance of love. Contrition is defined as "grief or sorrow for one's sins and shortcomings." When we are open to grace, we experience sorrow over our failures to please God but accept God's love for us in spite of these failures. So contrition and acceptance of love are crucial parts of openness to grace.

Contrition and Acceptance of Love

In exploring the genuineness of contrition and acceptance of love, I shall be dealing with matters that go to the root of human existence. Both contrition and acceptance of love collide with the motives that undercut singleness of heart, and these motives, as we have seen, permeate every area of our lives, both secular and religious. With them we have built up a sense of worth, and through them we have carved out an identity, both of which must crumble and be remade when we become open to God's grace. We can hardly help exposing ruined foundations when discussing contrition and acceptance of love.

Moreover, only with contrition and acceptance of love can we experience rebirth. Only these can root out self-congratulation and self-justification. Without them we cannot acquire a genuine sense of worth or secure self-acceptance. We need contrition and the awareness of being loved to quell our restless hearts and satisfy our longings for eternity.

First I shall describe what contrition and acceptance of love are not, then I shall describe what they are, and finally I shall describe their effects.

What Contrition and Acceptance of Love Are Not

Contrition and acceptance of love do not involve any of the motives that undermine singleness of heart. Our sorrow is not aimed at gaining anything other than receiving forgiveness, and our acceptance of love is not directed at anything other than being loved. Sorrow and acceptance of love are unconditional in the same way that grace is unconditional. God does not attach conditions to his grace, and we do not attach conditions to our openness to it.

(1) Being contrite and accepting love are not things we do or feel in order to obtain someone's admiration. We do not act contritely with the thought that God will admire us for doing so or with the thought that our Christian friends will admire us. We do not have an image of people smiling at us because they know we have been contrite. Nor do we expect anyone to voice approval for our having accepted God's forgiveness. We do not picture an audience listening with rapt attention as we describe our failings and the forgiveness we have received for them. We do not imagine our parents, minister, or friends approving of what we have done. And we do not think of ourselves as deserving recognition for possessing something that is highly praised by other Christians.

Feeling loved by God is not the same as the euphoria we have when we know others admire us. Because both involve contentment, a sense of well-being, and a degree of elation, we can mistake the euphoria for the feeling of being loved. Admiration, however, is based on our having certain qualities, but love is not. Our parents may admire us for our intelligence, attractiveness, or accomplishments, but they love us simply because we are their children. So our feeling of being loved by God is different from the feeling of being admired.

(2) We do not act contritely or accept love when we respond out of fear of what others would think if we were not to do so. If someone apologizes to us for a wrong done, we do not feel apologized to if we know that fear is the only motive for the apology. If, for instance, an employee wrongs us and apologizes because she is afraid of losing her job, we would look at her words simply as a means of saving herself. What she obtains from the accepted apology is not a sense of forgiveness but relief from fear. The same is true if we utter

words of apology to God out of fear of what he would do to us if we did not utter the words, or out of fear of what other Christians would think if they knew we did not utter the words.

It is not just words of apology that can be used to dispel fear; it is feelings of apology as well, or what we take to be feelings of apology. They too are nothing but relief from fear if their aim is to placate God or pacify our anxiety about what other Christians would think if they knew about our inner states.

(3) Contrition and acceptance of love are not achievements we can use to demonstrate our goodness or justify our existence. They are not possessions about which we can say, "I have these, so now God must regard me as good." We cannot use them to procure God's favor. Nor can we use them to make ourselves heroes. We cannot boast, either to others or to ourselves, that having them makes us special people.

We can mistake feelings of self-justification for feelings of being loved by God because both involve the sense that our existence is validated. With both we feel that our failings do not count against us. Self-justification, however, is based on achievement, but love is not, so the experience of the first is not the same as the experience of the second.

(4) Contrition and acceptance of love do not make us feel superior to others, for they are levelers, not discriminators. They do not raise us above the common level of humanity or cause us to feel distinguished. They do not allow us to think, "I am good and you are not. I have settled my destiny but you have not." They bring about a sense of solidarity with others, not differentiation.

(5) Being contrite and accepting love are not things we do or feel in order to admire ourselves. We do not accept God's love so that we can gratify our ego or increase our sense of self-importance for being associated with God, as we sometimes do with famous people with whom we are acquainted. Nor do we act contritely or accept love so that we can commend ourselves for pleasing God. When these motives control us, we are really engaging in self-admiration instead of accepting God's love.

(6) Being contrite and accepting love are not things other people can do for us. They are not experiences of a group with which we

identify and in which we are hidden. They are not derived from expectations of a group and do not result from our thinking of them as the things to have because the group has them. Nor are they products of other people's initiative. They are not, in short, someone else's experiences.

In addition to these six, which are connected to motives undermining singleness of heart, there are two other things that the contrition involved in being open to grace is not.

(7) The sorrow of contrition is not the same as despair.[2] Despair involves the feeling of irredeemable hopelessness. With despair we tell ourselves we cannot be forgiven or loved. We feel we cannot amend our habits or eliminate the pride that constantly afflicts us. We are stuck in a life we do not like, unable to get ourselves unstuck.

Although contrition involves a sense of hopelessness that is akin to helplessness, it is not the irredeemable sort, for contrition believes in possibility. It does not feel glued to habits and pride. It is willing to accept forgiveness and love. It may not accept love immediately or easily, but if in the end contrition is not conjoined with this acceptance, it is really despair.

(8) Contrition is also not the same as self-hate or self-condemnation.[3] It is not masochistic fascination with sin or obsessive brooding on the dark parts of our past. It is not self-loathing that wallows in suffering for sin, nor is it revenge against ourselves. It does not say, "I am a bad person, not worthy of being loved. My guilt is too much for anyone to forgive. I have to hate myself because that is what I deserve."

Again, true contrition comes with acceptance of love. This means we must accept ourselves as worthy of being loved. We cannot accept someone's love for us if we hate ourselves or feel intractably evil. Contrition is not a condemning attitude. It does not run from love but seeks it, for it wants healing, and healing can come only with the awareness of being loved. Self-hate drives wounds deeper.

---

2. Kierkegaard, *The Sickness unto Death,* trans. Howard V. Hong and Edna H. Hong (Princeton: Princeton University Press, 1980), pp. 111-12.

3. Max Scheler, "Repentance and Rebirth," in *On the Eternal in Man,* trans. Bernard Noble (New York: Harper, 1960), p. 53.

There are other attitudes that can be mistaken for openness to grace, such as excitement in Christian contexts or friendly feelings directed toward us by other Christians. Identifying these eight, however, is sufficient for getting to the core of what openness to grace is not. I turn now to a positive description of being open to grace.

What Contrition and Acceptance of Love Are

(1) Contrition is sadness mixed with regret and aversion. In their mild form these feelings produce quiet distress; in their extreme form they produce bitter suffering.

One way to pinpoint the sadness in contrition is to notice what it is like in situations not involving contrition. Grief at the premature death of a friend and sadness for victims of misfortune arise from the awareness that a situation is not as it could be. When we observe acquaintances wasting their lives, wandering aimlessly from job to job, we are sad for the same reason. We become dismayed when someone we know becomes schizophrenic, commits criminal acts, or crumbles under the weight of painful memories.

The sadness in contrition also arises from the awareness that a situation is not as it could be. The situation about which we are sad involves us, not someone else. Our grief springs from the fact that we have so often succumbed to fits of impatience. Our dismay comes from the realization that we have needlessly hurt someone we care deeply about. Our sorrow originates from knowing that we are not living the loving way we imagine we could.

Sadness is not the only element of contrition. If it were, contrition would not make us so uneasy. Sadness, to be sure, is distressing, but it does not produce the uneasiness that regret produces. Regret is added to sadness when we are conscious that the situation about which we are sad is one that we have brought about. We see that we have been responsible for substituting an imaginary Christianity for real Christianity. We notice that our indifference is not something that has happened to us but something that we have chosen. We perceive reluctantly that our secondhand faith is a tragedy of our own making.

93

The uneasiness in contrition becomes especially acute when we experience aversion toward what we have done. Aversion arises when we find the comparisons we indulge in distasteful. We turn away from them with disgust, along with a tinge of horror at the fact that we have done what we so detest in others.

The uneasiness in contrition also comes from the realization that we have let God down. His wish for us is that we live without ceaseless strivings to make ourselves better than everyone else. When we are conscious of this wish and also of our strenuous efforts to be superior, we feel keen discomfort. So we direct our contrition both toward ourselves and, in a way, toward God.

We also feel contrite about our wanting self-justification and not just our doing things to justify ourselves. A striking way to illustrate the difference between wanting and doing is by means of the Ten Commandments. We Christians are likely to have a hard time thinking of the Ten Commandments as being very pertinent to us because we do not lie, cheat, kill, or worship idols. Criminals are the ones who lie and cheat and kill, and pagans in primitive tribes worship idols. We cannot feel contrite about something we do not do, so our attitude toward the Commandments is likely to be that they are good for invoking contrition in non-Christians. But when we find ourselves in a difficult situation and the impulse to kill the person who is the source of the difficulty suddenly arises, and we relish the impulse momentarily, we cannot help but see that the Commandments are meant to invoke contrition in us, too.

It is the same with Paul's declaration, "For by grace you have been saved through faith, and this is not your own doing; it is the gift of God — not the result of works, so that no one may boast" (Eph. 2:8-9). We tell ourselves that we do not believe in justification by works; Paul is here writing to those who think their existence can be justified through what they do and not through God's grace. But telling ourselves this is a dodge to evade knowing how badly we want to justify ourselves by our achievements. Paul's statements are aimed both at those who believe in justification by works and at those who, though they do not officially believe in it, nevertheless want it. The sorrow, regret, and aversion of contrition are directed

94

toward having this want and toward the likings and desirings involved in other motives that undermine singleness of heart.

(2) Openness to grace also involves letting go of our attachment to motives that undermine singleness of heart, letting go of the identity we have fashioned on the basis of these motives, and letting go of the sense of worth we have based on this identity.

The letting go in being open to grace is like the letting go in certain situations that do not involve grace. We would be distraught if our wallet were stolen, if our car were totaled in an accident, or if a fire were to burn our house and everything in it. To dispel inner turbulence, we must, after giving ourselves time to grieve, let go of our attachment to the stolen wallet, the totaled car, or the destroyed home and furniture. We may think at first that we cannot live without these (and perhaps it may seem so for a time), but we will be able to go on if we emotionally disengage ourselves from them.

This disengagement is similar to what happens when we become open to grace. We give up things that we have dearly loved and let go of our fear that their loss will make life empty. We relinquish our hold on deep-seated attitudes. We detach ourselves from what we have clung to almost for life itself.

First, we let go of motives that produce dividedness. We abandon the striving and achieving we have used to justify our existence. We give up our need to be widely admired and our desire to assume the identity of a group. We break our attachment to the feeling that we have to be better than everyone else. We let go of our drive to be doing something all the time to avoid thinking about meaning, death, and isolation.

We also let go of the identity we have derived from our achievements and superiorities. We no longer think of ourselves as people who are always getting things done, because we have given up the drive that makes us always want to do things. We cease picturing ourselves as being admired by important people; this we have abandoned as self-justifying.

Last, in being open to grace we let go of the sense of worth we have gotten from the identity we have given up. We do not think of ourselves as having no worth; rather, we change its foundation.

Because we no longer cling to superiority and admiration, these do not serve as foundations. Neither do the Christian groups with which we have identified, or the accomplishments we have used to impress friends.

In each of these instances of letting go, something breaks. What breaks is our tight grip on the attitudes that have dominated our inner lives. Because these attitudes have been central to our self-concept, it is shattered when our grip on the attitudes breaks. What we conceive ourselves to be is so tied in to these attitudes that letting go of them is like letting go of our whole selves.

In each letting go there is also a melting of long-standing resistance. We have resisted letting go of the motives that produce dividedness. We have also resisted letting go of the self-concept based on these motives. Because the motives and the self-concept are so much a part of us, the resistance is as well. It has occupied a controlling place in our personalities. Melting it is, again, like melting our whole selves.

(3) A third feature of being open to grace is being receptive to the love God gives. To be receptive to love, we must not only be given it but must also consent to be given it. To see what is involved, consider several cases in which a person is a recipient of a gift but does not welcome receiving it. This can happen if she is alienated from the giver and wants to maintain distance. It can happen if she is independent and self-reliant, and feels that accepting a gift would make her dependent and helpless. It can happen if she feels she does not deserve to receive gifts because of low self-esteem or feelings of unworthiness. Or it can happen if she otherwise does not want a certain gift.

In these cases the receiver of the gift does not assent to being given it. Though she accepts the gift in one sense, she does not in another, for she does not feel it is really hers. She puts it into a drawer and forgets she has it or displays the gift simply out of politeness, but is indifferent or uncomfortable about having it.

On the other hand, a person who accepts a gift willingly delights in the fact that someone has done something nice for her. She feels that the gift is hers and experiences an inner warmth when she thinks about it.

When we are receptive to God's love, we give God permission

to give us something. We let God love us in the same way a willing recipient of a gift lets someone give her something. We do not distance ourselves from the love but feel that it belongs to us. We like having it.

Though letting God love us is something we do, we do not do anything to get it. We do not actively take the initiative as we do when we buy something or perform a task. Nor do we go after it in the way that we go after success and admiration. And we take it differently from the way we take a book off a shelf. All these involve self-initiated actions, whereas letting God love us involves permitting love to come to us.

In addition, we perceive that God's love comes to us without regard to our achievements and superior qualities. The love is not, we sense, a reward for them; they are not the reason it is given to us. We feel loved for the sake of the loving itself. The delight we experience when we receive God's love is not the same as the exhilaration we feel when we are awarded a prize for being the best. It is delight in the love only.

Moreover, we sense that God gives his love to us even though he knows about our secrets. God's love comes with an acceptance of us; it is not that he takes no notice of our secrets but that he knows about them and does not hold them against us. In receiving love, we accept this acceptance. We allow God to love us even though we are aware that he knows about our hidden desires.

Finally, we do not feel that having God's love distinguishes us from others, making us better than they are or worthy of their admiration. When we receive God's love, we have no thought of superiority or inferiority. We do not use that love to get a higher status. We receive it for no end other than to be loved.

The next two features of openness to grace are not part of its content, as the preceding three are, but characterize the way in which we are open to it.

(4) Perhaps the most prominent feature of being open to grace is the difficulty we experience in doing so. One initially thinks that being open to grace is easy because grace is freely offered and comes without conditions. We do not have to do anything to secure it. Yet Augustine characterizes God's mercy as "severe," and Jonathan Ed-

wards writes that we must "wrestle with God in prayer for mercy" if our hearts are to be awakened.[4] These are surprising ways to talk about mercy. However, if we look again at what is involved in being receptive to it, we will see that it has a severe quality and that it does require wrestling.

(a) In order to have the sorrow of contrition, we must admit that we have acted in order to be admired and that we have secretly commended ourselves for loving the unlovable. We must admit these both to ourselves and to the One from whom we receive love.

This admission is one source of the wrestling that openness to grace requires, for we are desperate to protect what goes on inside us both from ourselves and from others. Partners in crime might revel in their criminal adventures; we too might reveal our secrets if we knew they would be admired. But to confess, knowing that we are admitting failure, is almost terrifying. Ernest Becker writes, "Everything painful and sobering in what psychoanalytic genius and religious genius have discovered about man revolves around the terror of admitting what one is doing to earn his self-esteem."[5] We cannot admit this in an offhanded or dismissive way.

(b) Another source of grace's severity is the letting go that contrition requires. The desires to compare, to commend ourselves, and to use people are exceedingly strong. We like these desires immensely and are enormously gratified when they are satisfied. We have become so used to satisfying them that they have become like comfortable habits. Our first impulse when we meet new people is to impress them; we constantly use socially approved roles to justify our existence.

These habits possess more power over us than everyday habits such as coffee drinking and television watching because they involve more than just everyday likes. They involve desires that affect what we

---

4. Augustine, *Confessions,* trans. John K. Ryan (New York: Doubleday–Image Books, 1960), Book 8, Chapter 11, p. 200; and Edwards, *Treatise on Religious Affections,* p. 102.

5. Becker, *The Denial of Death* (New York: Macmillan–The Free Press, 1973), p. 6.

conceive to be the core of our identity, desires that we regard as indispensable to our very existence. Giving them up is a good deal more difficult than giving up everyday habits because we cannot do so without tearing ourselves apart. Augustine recognized the power of habit and the process by which desire becomes habit. Using the desire with which he wrestled most as an example, he wrote, "In truth, lust is made out of a perverse will, and when lust is served, it becomes habit, and when habit is not resisted, it becomes necessity."[6] It is not too much to say that we are addicted to using other people.

Our wrestling with grace can be illustrated by what goes on when we criticize people, whether we make the criticism openly or to ourselves. Doing so gives us the pleasure of thinking that we are better than others. This incites us to continue criticizing whenever the opportunity presents itself. Habit soon ensnares us, and a critical attitude arises automatically whenever we observe someone else's ineptness or failure. With time this critical attitude comes to feel natural. We need it to feel secure. Because of its entrenchment, we resist admitting we have it. We also resist the application of grace to it because we see that we would have to give up our desire to have the attitude. When grace triumphs in the end, we exchange our critical attitude for acceptance and love, but not without heart-wrenching struggle.

(c) A last source of wrestling with grace comes from the uneasiness we experience when we receive love. Ingrained within us is a system of reward and punishment that is based on the concept of desert. When we do something good, we instinctively feel that we should be rewarded; when we do something bad, we feel just as instinctively that we should be punished (though we also want to avoid punishment). To set aside this system, as love does, is to violate this deeply implanted sense of moral order. We feel we do not deserve to be loved, so we push love away (even though we want it). We cannot bear being loved by someone whom we think believes that we do not deserve it. To let ourselves be loved by such a person is like receiving a gift from an acquaintance whom we have let down. We want to give it back.

6. Augustine, *Confessions,* Book 8, Chapter 5, p. 188.

There is something else that makes us want to give back God's love. The validation that love brings collides with the justification we get from our achievements and admirable qualities. Love's validation disregards these, so that we feel we have wasted our lives in pursuing self-justifying projects. We can scarcely endure this upheaval of a lifetime of efforts to make ourselves into something significant.

In Dostoyevksy's *Crime and Punishment*, Raskalnikov feels the sting of love after he confesses the murder he has committed to Sonia. "The two sat side by side, mournful and dejected, as though they had been washed up alone on a deserted shore after a storm. He looked at Sonia and sensed how much her love was on him; strangely, it suddenly felt weary and painful to be loved like that — a strange and terrible sensation!" Before he confessed, "he had thought he would be able to unload at least part of his torment, and now, all of a sudden, when she turned to him with all her heart, he suddenly felt and realized that he was infinitely more miserable than he had been before."[7]

Chauntecleer, the Lord Rooster in Walter Wangerin's *The Book of Sorrows*, feels the sting of love so much that he rejects it. When the Dun Cow rescues him from drowning and breathes warm breath onto him, he senses he is being given undeserved love. "What a terrible thing loving is!" he exclaims to himself. Chauntecleer realizes that he both wants and does not want this love. "The pain was that the less he deserved her love, the more he desired it." When the Dun Cow says, "Look at me," Chauntecleer finds that he cannot. He finally says, "Go away," and the Dun Cow leaves.[8]

Both Raskalnikov and Chauntecleer have discovered firsthand that letting themselves be loved is harder than they originally imagined — harder than uncovering the darkness within, harder than confessing this darkness to another, harder even than loving itself.

(5) Despite the arduousness of being open to grace, we want

7. Dostoyevsky, *Crime and Punishment*, trans. Sidney Monas (New York: New American Library, 1968), p. 409.

8. Wangerin, Jr., *The Book of Sorrows* (New York: Harper & Row, 1985), pp. 61-62.

the state to continue. Almost in spite of ourselves, we feel ourselves being drawn to the sorrow, the letting go, and the receiving of love. We recollect prior experiences of these and let them expand inside us. They awaken a desire for more of the same.

This desire involves both habit and inclination. Letting God love us becomes a habit, not by virtue of being involuntary and automatic, but by being regular and frequent. The habit here is more like a voluntary custom that we renew each time we repeat what we do. It is a habit of wanting. We want to receive love again; we possess a continual appetite for it. We also want, in a sense, new occasions of sorrow and letting go. Painful though these are, we see them as fitting and required by the taking in of love.[9]

Developing a desire for fresh experiences of grace makes us become aware of the centrality of grace in the life of the Christian. Being conscious of grace, feeling it, and letting it direct our motives, both conscious and unconscious, come to dominate our lives. We want grace to sink into the deepest parts of ourselves. Our aim is to be so thoroughly permeated by grace that we do not overtly act in Christian ways while secretly pursuing reward and self-justification.

Our conception of Christian activities changes too. We realize that performance and achievement are not the essence of Christian existence but that receiving and giving grace are. Visits to church become occasions for new episodes of sorrow, letting go, and receiving of love.

It is important to note that the desire for new episodes of sorrow is not a desire for continuous sorrow. Continuous sorrow can produce despair; it can undercut Christian joy and make us dark and melancholic. Perpetual sorrow indicates the presence of self-absorption, which can cause us to retreat into ourselves and withdraw from grace-giving interaction. Although the life of the Christian is a life of sorrow, it is also a life of delight and giving. "Grief for sins is necessary, but must not be perpetual," observes

---

9. "The degree of religion is rather to be judged of by the fixedness and strength of the habit that is exercised in affection, whereby holy affection is habitual, than by the degree of the present exercise" (Edwards, *Treatise on Religious Affections*, p. 118).

Bernard. "My advice is to turn back at times from sorrow and the anxious remembrance of your ways, and escape to the plain, to a calm review of the divine mercies. Let us mingle honey with wormwood. . . . While you think humbly of yourselves, think also of the goodness of the Lord."[10] One who is open to grace yields to sorrow but also moves beyond sorrow.

The case is different for receiving love, which we can scarcely experience too much. Love stills our turbulent emotions, heals sorrow's wounds, and evicts self-justification. Continuously experiencing love, unlike continuously experiencing sorrow, is not an indication of being self-absorbed, for love draws us out of ourselves. It creates an enlivening delight that spills over. We want to give ourselves away when we experience God's acceptance.

The Effects of Being Open to Grace

To test the genuineness of feelings and attitudes, we must, in addition to inspecting them directly, observe their effects, both on other inner states and on our behavior. When feelings change or increase in intensity, the inner states and behavior to which they are connected also change. This is especially true of contrition and acceptance of love. They are so closely connected to so many feelings, attitudes, and ways of acting that they alter significant parts of our personalities.

Max Scheler noticed this fact about repentance. Rebirth, he said, is not a "dispensable and inessential" by-product of repentance. A change of heart is a natural result of "a soul which has yielded itself to be cleansed from guilt. . . . There is no Repentance which does not from its inception enclose the blueprint of a new heart."[11]

One significant effect of being open to grace is that the direction of the energy we expend changes. Before we become open to grace,

---

10. Bernard, Cant. Setto. xi, quoted by John Calvin in *Institutes of the Christian Religion,* trans. Henry Beveridge (Grand Rapids: Wm. B. Eerdmans, 1957), vol. 1, p. 521 (3.3.15).

11. Scheler, "Repentance and Rebirth," pp. 56-57.

our life's energy is directed toward securing favorable attitudes from others, resisting self-knowledge, and building up an edifice of self-justifying accomplishments to ward off the ever-present sense of unworth. We push ourselves to do things we know we and others will admire. We devote our inner resources to maintaining an image of being the kind of person who is in control of life, who is good, and who in Christian contexts does the right Christian things.

After becoming open to grace, we quit striving to be better than everyone else and work on accepting ourselves even if we know someone else is superior. We stop using people for ego enhancement and adopt need-free attitudes toward them. We give up false fronts and become more open.

The change here involves not only a redirection of energy; it also involves a release from old ways of expending energy and a freedom to engage in new ways. As we let go of motives that produce dividedness, we become aware of having been lured and trapped by them. We feel that they have driven us. Becoming open to grace frees us from this drivenness.[12] We can now be nonjudgmental and encouraging, tender and caring, without needing to use these to get something in return. We can smile, pray, and attend church without feeling we must do so to keep up appearances. We can open ourselves to God without having to protect ourselves from him.[13]

The redirection and release together make up the transformation that accepting grace causes. We no longer hide from ourselves or keep busy hiding from God. The newness we shrank from when contemplating grace ceases to be frightening, and the largeness of single-minded love is no longer overwhelming. Gratitude springs up in us spontaneously. So does sensitivity to others' feelings. We become interested in what acquaintances are doing and value knowing about it without succumbing to envy. We accept those who are

12. "You are now *free* from the floodtide of bygone guilt and wickedness that was sweeping you relentlessly away" (Scheler, "Repentance and Rebirth," p. 42).

13. "Repentance . . . enables life to begin, with a spontaneous, virginal beginning, a new course springing forth from the centre of the personality which, by virtue of the act of repentance, is no longer in bonds" (Scheler, "Repentance and Rebirth," p. 42).

different even if we think their beliefs are wrong. We accept ourselves, too. We can say, "I am loved," and find in this a secure basis
for a sense of worth.[14]

Part of the greatness of Dostoyevsky's *Crime and Punishment* is
that it makes the reader identify with the characters in it. When
Raskalnikov is driven by a murderous impulse, the reader feels the
same impulse plus the torturous depression Raskalnikov undergoes
as a result of the murder he commits. When Raskalnikov cannot eat
because of his inner tumult, when he can scarcely sleep and wildly
roams the streets of St. Petersburg, the reader too feels this confused
agitation. The same is true when at last Raskalnikov confesses, receives love, and senses something new taking hold of him. "The
blind melancholy and anxiety of the recent past, but especially of
the last few hours, oppressed him to such a degree that he simply
plunged into the possibility of this new, whole and complete sensation. It came upon him suddenly like a kind of nervous fit; took fire
first as a single spark in his soul, and suddenly, like flame, seized
everything. Everything seemed to melt inside him, and tears flowed.
He dropped to the earth where he stood."[15]

A Cry for Mercy

Carolyn was a devout Christian, regular in her church attendance
and well liked by those who knew her. As a child she had memorized
numerous verses from the Bible, many of which she would call to
mind from time to time. When asked to lead a Bible study one year,
she did so. Each Sunday she put her offering envelope into the plate
as it passed her. Unlike Raskalnikov, she possessed no wild tempera-
ment; on occasion she exhibited a certain softness that was touching
to its recipients.

---

14. "Trying to calculate one's moral worth by reference to human standards
leads to disquietude and doubt of self, never to certainty and self-assurance" (Louis
Mackey, *Kierkegaard: A Kind of Poet* [Pittsburgh: University of Pennsylvania Press,
1971], p. 87).

15. Dostoyevsky, *Crime and Punishment*, p. 505.

On the Sunday morning during which the following incident took place, Carolyn had gone to church as usual and had sat in her regular spot about two-thirds of the way back on the right. Not long after the service started, she realized that the cold she had gotten the day before was beginning to make her uncomfortable. Her headache had increased since she had left home, she began to feel achy, and she could scarcely keep her eyes open. Her discomfort was not bad enough to make her get up and leave (she would have been too embarrassed to do so anyway), but it was preventing her from getting much out of the service. So she decided that this once she would not pay attention to what was going on. If anything soaked in, that would be okay, but if nothing did, it would not matter because she really should be home in bed.

The thought occurred to her that although she was not able to be present to her surroundings, she could pray. This would make the morning useful, and it would make the time go by more quickly. She soon discovered, however, that she did not have the energy to do even this. Her mind could not do the confessing, thanking, praising, and interceding that a decent prayer was supposed to do. All she could do was sit with a blank mind and wait for the service to end.

She remembered reading about a prayer called "The Jesus Prayer," which said, "Lord Jesus Christ, have mercy on me." Ancient Christians had prayed this short prayer continually. She had thought this practice rather odd because it seemed to her that one meaningful confession should be enough. She herself had made such a confession and did not feel a need to do it repeatedly, as had been recommended by the author of the book in which she had found the prayer. But boredom was setting in, so Carolyn repeated the words in her mind, not as a prayer, but as something to keep her mind busy. She pretended to be listening to what was going on, she stood to sing, and she bowed her head when the minister prayed, all the while saying those words to herself.

The first several dozen repetitions soothed her. About the fifth or sixth dozen time, something began to happen. Whereas at first she had felt that she had control over her repetition of the prayer, she now began to feel that she could not stop saying it. The words

105

kept coming without her voluntary effort. It was something inside her, she noticed, that moved them along, but it seemed to be something outside her as well.

In addition, she began to feel the words digging into her. At first they had been more or less inert, but now they started doing things, things which she felt afraid of. They were uncovering material she didn't want uncovered. They were shoving aside barriers, tossing out carefully constructed defenses, and rummaging around in places she had thought were private.

She started to get up so she could escape, but an impending sense of embarrassment held her to the pew. How could she tell people what she was running from?

". . . and there is more . . . ," the minister's voice said, breaking into her inner drama. "There is more," she thought. The words inside her suddenly stopped, and for a moment she wondered what was going to happen next. What happened was that she said the words again: "Lord Jesus Christ, have mercy on me." This time they came voluntarily. They did not dig or uncover or toss out, but moved into her with an infinitely engaging softness. She let them do this; she allowed them to touch the places into which she had deposited her secrets. She let them touch the secrets themselves. A lump welled up in her throat, and an intense sense of release and awakening spread through her.

"So that's what mercy is," she exclaimed to herself with surprised wonder. The expanding newness she felt made her want to embrace someone and be embraced in return. She continued to sit, breathing easily and freely, waiting until she could get up and look into the eyes of those around her with a depth she had not hitherto possessed.

Chapter 7

A Community of Grace

*Happy are the simple followers of Jesus Christ who have been
overcome by his grace, and are able to sing the praises of the
all-sufficient grace of Christ with humbleness of heart. . . .
Happy are they who know that discipleship simply means the
life which springs from grace, and that grace simply means
discipleship.*

Dietrich Bonhoeffer, *The Cost of Discipleship*

*A reasonable soul cannot be without love while it is in this life
. . . for to love and be loved is the secret business of all human
life.*

Richard Rolle, *The Fire of Love*

In Chapter Three I described a number of motives that undermine
singleness of heart. In this chapter I shall describe how a community of grace can counteract these motives and their effects on our
interaction with others. We possess, or can possess, a drive for grace
— the desire both to give and to receive grace from others in a
human community. This desire helps drive off both the ambivalence
and the illusion that the undermining motives bring about. Our lot

is not so bleak as Chapter Three's survey of "nongrace" motives seems to indicate.

To describe how the giving and the receiving of grace take place in a community of grace, I will ask, first, what it would be like to be tax collectors who give grace, and, second, what it would be like to be Pharisees who are given grace. This procedure is suggested by the imaginative identification with others that is embodied in the Golden Rule. If we are to act toward others as we want them to act toward us, we have to imagine how we would react if we were someone else being treated in a certain way. We can also use this imaginative reconstruction of someone else's inner states to discover our own feelings and attitudes; it can, on occasion, be more revealing than straightforward introspection. What would we feel if we were tax collectors giving grace to Pharisees? How would we react if we were Pharisees being given grace by, of all people, tax collectors?

There is another reason for asking these questions. If we belong to a community of grace, we actually are tax collectors and Pharisees. We are Pharisees who need to receive grace, and we are tax collectors who can give grace. The central feature of a community of grace is this giving and receiving. Those in such a community think of themselves and of others in the community as both tax collectors and Pharisees. By imagining ourselves to be grace-giving tax collectors and grace-receiving Pharisees, therefore, we are doing more than conceiving of a hypothetical situation; we are investigating an actual community of grace.

Grace-Giving Tax Collectors

Imagine, first, that we are tax collectors. Tax collectors in biblical times were resented by the people of Israel for two reasons. First, they were collectors of a tax that was imposed upon Israel by the Romans. Because the Israelites resented the tax, they resented those who collected it. Second, tax collectors often padded the imposed tax with an additional amount for themselves, which they used to live sumptuously. The Israelites may have resented this surtax even more.

If we were tax collectors, then, we would feel this double resentment coming at us. We would not feel accepted in the homes or congregations of the Israelites. We would be especially uncomfortable in the presence of Pharisees, whose reputation as good, religious people was well established. We would be aware of the judgment in their behavior toward us and of the disapproval both of our official position and of our skimming.

But, being tax collectors, we would also have stood on the other side of the street (because we would not have been welcome at the Pharisees' worship services) and, without bowing our heads or closing our eyes, would have prayed not a publicly acceptable prayer but one springing from a desperate desire to find forgiving love: "God, be merciful to me, a sinner." We would also desire to act toward others with the same mercy that God gave us. We would even be moved, somewhat to our astonishment, to act in this way toward Pharisees.

The question is, then, How would we feel and act toward Pharisees if we were to give them grace? What attitudes would we have toward them, and what particular things would we do? Although the alienation between tax collectors and Pharisees in Israel prevented the kind of interchanges between them that I am envisaging, I shall imagine that there is interaction and shall refer to tax collectors and Pharisees as Christians. I shall begin by describing some things we would not do or feel.

In the first place, we would not tell Pharisees that people are sinners, that God forgives sinners and transforms them into new persons, and that he does so when they confess their sin and ask for forgiveness. We would not point out to them that God hates pride and self-righteousness but loves meekness and humility. We would particularly not quote passages from the Bible that we think are pertinent to the condition of Pharisees. Nor would we suggest that they read certain books or go to certain churches. We would not do these things because we would know that Pharisees are already acquainted with the concepts of sin and forgiveness. They are, of all religious people, the most knowledgeable about the Bible and the most well-read. They would be the first to tell us, known sinners, that God requires confession and repentance. They love to talk about theological truths with each other and spend time reading books on Christian subjects. So we would realize that it would be pointless to engage in these activities with Pharisees; if they have not received grace by means of them before, they probably will not receive grace by means of them now.

Moreover, a repetition of their beloved truths would be likely to entrench Pharisees further in their familiar illusions. Although they would reaffirm the ancient truths with relish and vigor as the words God himself is speaking, they would use them to hide from themselves or to compare themselves with those who do not affirm the truths or who do not affirm them as vigorously as they themselves do. They have done these things for so long that it is likely that they would continue to do them. So, we would realize, not only would it be pointless to preach genuine Christianity to Pharisees to try to awaken them from what we conceive to be their false Christianity, but it probably would reinforce their unknowing self-justification.

In addition, if we were tax collectors giving grace to Pharisees, we would not tell them that they admire themselves for their Christian goodness. We would not point out the inconsistency between their public posture and their inner reality. We would not tell them that they are using other Christians to enhance their sense of self-importance or that they constantly compare themselves with others. We would not say these things, though they might be true, because the recipients of our assertions would react defensively in the strongest manner possible. Their response would be to affirm their upright character, which everyone else but us is able to see. Besides, they would say, you tax collectors should learn how to be good Christians before you start attacking other Christians. These reactions, we realize, would drive Pharisees further from the grace that we wish them to receive.

There is a more important reason why as tax collectors we would not say these things to Pharisees. In spite of our honest and sincere intentions, these declarations are judgmental. If they were directed at us, we would feel condemned. But because we have been given forgiving love, our attitude toward Pharisees is not one of condemnation. It is an entirely different attitude that involves several features.

It involves, first, the knowledge that although Pharisees appear to be unafraid and unhurt, they really have the same fears and wounds that we do. These fears and wounds are hidden behind the armor of character they have constructed. The purpose of the public character of Pharisees, their ostensive Christian virtue and observable piety, is to ward off the feeling that they are not good enough. They use it to protect themselves from intrusion and to prevent themselves from feeling apprehensive about not measuring up to accepted standards. Pharisees do not notice that they are doing this.[1] We notice, however (because we have done it ourselves), and when we do, our attitude changes from condemnation to compassion. Our intense aversion toward those who are putting on a show is replaced by empathy because we realize that they, like us, are trying to stave off inner pain.

In addition, our attitude as tax collectors would involve giving Pharisees what we believe they need, not what we know they want. We know they want to be admired for their observance of accepted Christian practice. They want to use their interactions with others to build their already oversized egos; they want to put themselves higher in the ranking system they use when they compare themselves with us. These, however, are not what we believe they need. We believe they need to have their armor of character punctured and their wounds tenderly touched. We believe they need the same forgiving love that we ourselves have received. It is these things we want to give to them, and not the admiration and esteem that feeds their voracious appetite for self-justification.

Lastly, our attitude toward Pharisees would involve wanting to give them gifts without desiring to get anything for doing so. We would not give so that we could receive respect from the Pharisees to whom we give or from those whom we know would notice. We would not give in order to congratulate ourselves for being gracious to those who act condescendingly toward us. We would give simply to be giving, because we believe it is intrinsically good to do so, and because we know that Pharisees need to be given to.

---

1. "Each of us is encased in an armour which we soon, out of familiarity, no longer notice" (Martin Buber, *Between Man and Man,* cited in *Four Existentialist Theologians,* ed. Will Herberg [New York: Doubleday, 1958], p. 180).

How, then, can we give grace to Pharisees? Notice that this question is not the same as asking what Pharisees must do to receive grace. As we shall see, they may not receive as grace what we give as grace. They may, in fact, never in their whole lives receive anything as grace even though they are given it countless times. We cannot do more than give, though we can be alert to what would and what would not be received as grace. Our question thus becomes, How can we give grace to Pharisees in ways that they will receive as grace? There is no absolutely certain answer to this question, but there are ways of giving grace that are more likely to be received as grace. I shall mention four.

One way is to touch — on the shoulder, on the elbow, with an arm around the shoulders, in the palm of the hand when we give some small object. As we touch, we intend for the recipients to feel loved with the same kind of love they felt when they were nurtured as children. We think of them as helpless infants who need to be held, which is how we secretly sometimes feel. We cannot, of course, hold Pharisees in the way we hold children, but we can touch them and convey a warm feeling of being loved no matter what.

Another way is to greet things not normally praised with unsolicited affirmation, praise, or expressions of delight. We typically praise others for public accomplishments or significant successes. But if we praised Pharisees for less noticeable things, we would be showing that we like them without regard for their superior talent or overt Christian practice. We can, for example, compliment them for the distinctive way they do some everyday activity: "I like the way you've arranged the furniture in this room" or "You write such wonderful letters to me!" These compliments certainly can bring about ego-expansive gratification and are indeed likely to do so in those who soak up praise or who invest their esteem-seeking energy in furniture arranging or letter writing. But these compliments can also produce a sense of being affirmed simply for oneself, especially in those who do not desire public recognition for these activities.

Still another way to give grace is to listen. When we listen to other people, we show that we want to know what they are feeling and thinking, what special projects they have been engaging in, or how they like their jobs. In showing that we want to know these things, we are telling others that we value them. By giving them our time and interest, we convey positive regard based not on the goodness they use for self-justification but on their intrinsic worth.

A fourth way to give grace is to confess our struggles, doubts, fears, and uncertainties, the wounds we have received and the pain we feel as a result. We must be careful here, for confessing is not so much a way of giving grace as it is of doing something fitting that can bring about the reception of grace in listeners. If we confess in order to get listeners to confess as well, we are really manipulating them. Our attitude must be the same as it is with giving; we confess without expecting anything in return other than gracious acceptance.

The kind of confession that can move listeners to receive grace is not the sort we engage in when we confess to God. We do not ask Pharisees for forgiveness. Rather, we admit things that we do not ordinarily want to admit to anyone. We might say, "The thing that most gets in the way of my living as a Christian is my busyness. It makes me feel as if I'm running from God when I really don't mean to." Or, "I've been discouraged lately because I'm not sure what direction my life has."

Not only do these admissions help heal those who confess, but they have a remarkably strong effect on the ones who listen. Unlike the impersonal assertion "Lack of direction causes discouragement," a personal admission stirs listeners to look closely inside themselves to see if they too are discouraged. With such admissions, what has hitherto gone undetected or unacknowledged in listeners can come to the surface. In addition, listeners feel safe in making candid confessions in return. By trusting listeners with their feelings, those who confess create an atmosphere of acceptance. This atmosphere undercuts the need for Pharisees to have an armor of character. If they feel the atmosphere, they also feel that they can set aside their armor and admit (to themselves at least) their fears, wounds, and self-justifying motives. The atmosphere is an atmosphere of grace, and the Pharisees' admissions are the beginnings of accepting grace.

Grace-Receiving Pharisees

Now let us imagine that we are Pharisees. Before asking what we would have to do to receive the tax collectors' grace, let us imagine ourselves reacting negatively toward it. We are the kind of Pharisees, let us suppose, who not only have no desire for grace but resist it when it is offered to us. We feel right with God because of our accomplishments, both secular and religious. We love being admired by other Pharisees, and we secretly admire ourselves for the correctness of our Christian attitudes and the depth of our Christian experience. We conceive ourselves to be superior (without being haughty, however) both to those in the church — particularly hypocrites, whom we discover almost instinctively and for whom we have a special dislike — and to those outside the church, especially wealth-amassing business people and those indifferent to matters of eternity. What we like most is for others to notice us and praise us. We especially like indications that we are esteemed for our Christian goodness and that others approve of our Christian practice. Our sense of worth comes from this esteem and approval.

If we are Pharisees of this sort, we clearly will not receive the tax collectors' grace as grace. One obstacle to doing so will be our lack of respect for tax collectors. People who give us things, we feel, have to be generally respected. If they are not respected, the attention we get from them means little to us. This shows that what we really want from the attention is something beyond it; we use the attention instead of simply receiving it.

Our grace-resisting reaction to the tax collectors' touching will be to see it as an affirmation of our importance. We think of being touched as the lesser admiring the greater, so the tax collectors' touching will separate us from them even further. Being given affirmation for things not normally praised will not be different for us than being praised for our public successes. We will use the former in the same self-justifying way we use the latter. It is admiration we will take in, not the tax collectors' attitude of acceptance. The thrill of talking and the sense of superiority we will feel when being listened to will keep the tax collectors' positive regard from getting through. As they are confessing their struggles, we will be admiring ourselves for being trusted enough by others for them to reveal their secrets to us. Perhaps, too, we will think of them as being inferior for having problems. And if, for an instant, we feel that what the tax collectors are admitting might be something with which we can identify, we will quickly drive off the feeling for fear that it will lead someplace we do not want it to.

If we are grace-resisting Pharisees, then, there is nothing we cannot use for our own gain. We can convert explicit grace-giving actions into reward, self-congratulation, or self-justification. It is possible for us to live in a grace-giving environment without our sensing it as one.

Now let us ask what would have to happen for us to receive the tax collectors' grace. First, we would have to consider tax collectors to be our equals. Or, rather, we would have to consider ourselves to be their equals. We could not think of them as inferior, for then it would be admiration we would be receiving from them and not grace. We would have to think of gifts from them as having equal value to those from Pharisees, but at the same time we could not think of these gifts as having the self-enhancing value we obtain from Pharisees' gifts. We would have to receive the tax collectors' gifts in the same "nongain" way they are given.

We would also have to have the same attitude toward ourselves that tax collectors have toward us — that we are wounded and hurt, fearing others' disapproval, and doubting our worth. We would have to see ourselves as lonely, as being afraid to love, as wrestling with the sharp jabs of conscience, as having unmentionable thoughts and fantasies, as people who want intensely to tell someone about our quiet desperation yet who are even more fearful of doing so. To receive the tax collectors' grace, we would have to notice that we have erected our virtuous public character to hide these wounds and fears, both from ourselves and from others, especially other Pharisees.

In addition, we would have to see that we have been driven by the desire for self-justification and that this desire has caused us to exhibit Christian goodness. Only if we noticed these things about ourselves could we receive the tax collectors' touching as an expression of love, their affirmation as acceptance not based on our public virtue, and their listening as a demonstration of positive regard for us. Only by becoming aware of our desire to justify ourselves could we identify with the confessions of the tax collectors, feel the atmosphere of trust created by them, and be stirred to probe our inner lives further.

Living in a Community of Grace

This imaginative reconstruction shows that thinking of ourselves as both tax collectors and Pharisees jolts us into recognizing our need for grace. It also shows that thinking of others as both tax collectors and Pharisees makes us realize that they too need grace. We become aware of our dependence upon others and of their dependence upon us for experiencing God's grace.[2]

A number of things take place in a community of grace. Perhaps the most prominent is that we become able to admit our secrets to others without fearing that they will reject us, and they become able to admit their secrets to us without fearing that we will reject them. We can confess that we have been active in church simply to be admired and that we have been addicted to success. We are able to acknowledge that behind our happy facades are wounded hearts that need to be loved. We can disclose our Christian pretensions without fear of disapproval.

The reason that we can make these disclosures is that the atmosphere in a community of grace is one of unconditional acceptance. This atmosphere is not just implicit; it is continually explicit in how we act toward each other and in what we say to each other. And it is something we are always working to foster, not just something we take for granted.

One of the effects of this atmosphere is that we are incited to be in a state of grace toward ourselves. When we know that others accept us, we begin to accept ourselves. Negative attitudes toward

2. "Creatures are placed in my way so that I, their fellow-creature, by means of them and with them, find the way to God" (Martin Buber, *Between Man and Man,* cited in *Four Existentialist Theologians,* p. 240).

ourselves cease to pervade our consciousness. We become able to live with the one person we are least able either to live with or to live without.

In addition, our need to admire ourselves is undercut. When we are in a state of grace toward ourselves, we do not need to use self-admiration to dispel our sense of unworth. The same is true for the need to justify ourselves and to compare ourselves with others. These lose their hold on us when the grace of the community works its way into us.

This grace also breaks through our numbness. When we are part of a group in which there is an active effort to diffuse a sense of grace, we are less likely simply to go through the motions of being Christians. Contrition becomes something we feel and not just something about which we have concepts. Going to church services becomes less a way of getting drugged and more a way of intensifying our spiritual perceptions.

Because we are constantly reminded of grace in a community of grace, we do not forget so easily that grace exists. Our grasp of this central dimension of Christian existence is not so precarious as it normally is. We are conscious of it more often, delight to receive it, and actively think of ways we can give it to others.

Perhaps the church is the most obvious place for a community of grace. Churches, however, are sometimes permeated with comparison, self-justification, and fear of disapproval, and thus do little to foster grace. The family is also an obvious place for giving and receiving grace, but families, like churches, often have little of it, marred as they are by criticism and indifference. One natural response to these realities is to view them with an attitude of distancing superiority; we do not do things that contaminate Christian communities, we tell ourselves. Another natural response is to want to leave and find a church where there is more grace or a family in which there is more warmth.

A different kind of response is to view those whom we think of as graceless Christians in the same way we view ourselves: as hurting individuals who need to be loved. This response makes us, in a sense, missionaries to other Christians. It also makes us bringers of grace to our spouses, family members, and co-workers. We can,

117

in short, create a community of grace; we do not need to go looking for one. In fact, if our only attitude toward a community of grace is that we must go looking for one in order to be part of one, we will never be part of one.

It is important to keep in mind that a community of grace is not a utopia. A utopia exists when a group of people has no shortcomings. A community of grace, however, contains people who want to be known as better than everyone else in the group, who use others in the group for their own gain, and who resist God's love while publicly declaring it. The distinctive feature of a community of grace is not perfection but the giving and the receiving of grace. This feature is what moves its members toward sensing eternity with less ambivalence and illusion.

Chapter 8

Beyond the Self

Nothing is so beautiful and wonderful, nothing is so continually
fresh and surprising, so full of sweet and personal ecstasy, as
the good. No desert is so dreary, monotonous and boring as
evil.

Simone Weil

Why were the eyes of little Nell wet, that night, with tears like
those of the two sisters? Why did she bear a grateful heart
because they had met, and feel it pain to think that they would
shortly part? Let us not believe that any selfish reference —
unconscious though it might have been — to her own trials
awoke this sympathy, but thank God that the innocent joys of
others can strongly move us, and that we, even in our fallen
nature, have one source of pure emotion which must be prized
in Heaven!

Charles Dickens, *The Old Curiosity Shop*

"Countless people experience their existence as dull, boring,
stagnant, and routine. They lack inner vitality, a deep desire

to be alive."[1] Many of us can identify with these observations by Henri Nouwen. We feel ourselves unthinkingly going through each day's activities with little enthusiasm for what we do. Life becomes tiresome, and we constantly plan how to obtain some compensating excitement.

We might think that if we could recapture the spontaneous wonderment of a child opening a gift, we would drive off our boredom. Or if we could experience every now and then an energizing expansiveness, the kind we felt when we first fell in love or when we received praise for an accomplishment, our drab existence would be brightened.

Though we often want to eliminate the dullness of our life in self-centered ways, we also yearn to escape self-centeredness. Something in us recognizes that, despite our insatiable appetite for self-satisfaction, we need to look outside ourselves. We feel that if we could do this, the hollowness we sense would be filled.

There are two other-focused ways of possessing singleness of heart that satisfy this yearning to be drawn out of ourselves: offering self-forgetful praise to God and being aware of moral beauty in people. Both of these give us quiet exhilaration and evoke childlike wonderment in us. They quell our restlessness and dispel the dull drudgery that seeps into our bones. They also infuse in us the "deep desire to be alive" that Nouwen refers to.

A dramatic instance of this last point involved a man I know named Alan. Several years ago, when I introduced him to the idea of moral beauty, I did not know that he had been planning to kill himself. His response at the time was rather blunt: "Isn't there evil in everyone? How can we see beauty in people?" Four months later, at the end of the summer, he mentioned that he had decided earlier in the year to drown himself during the summer. He had chosen drowning, he said, because he wasn't a very good swimmer, so his death would look like an accident. But in the end he decided not to go through with his plan. "What made you change your mind?" I asked. "It was those thoughts about moral beauty," he replied.

1. Nouwen, *Lifesigns: Intimacy, Fecundity and Ecstasy in Christian Perspective* (Garden City, N.Y.: Doubleday, 1986), p. 55.

In this chapter I shall describe these two ways in which we can have singleness of heart. They involve an other-directedness that contrasts both with self-centeredness and with legitimate self-regard.

Offering Self-forgetful Praise

As we read the Psalms, we encounter two kinds of praise. In the first, the Psalmist praises God for what God has done for him: "I will extol you, O Lord, for you have drawn me up, and did not let my foes rejoice over me" (30:1); "Bless the Lord, O my soul, and do not forget all his benefits — who forgives all your iniquity, who heals all your diseases, who redeems your life from the Pit, who crowns you with steadfast love and mercy, who satisfies you with good as long as you live so that your youth is renewed like the eagle's" (103:2-5). In these passages there is an explicit link between the author's praise and what the author receives from God. This link is absent in such passages as "Sing to the Lord a new song, his praise in the assembly of the faithful" (149:1) and "Praise the Lord, for the Lord is good; sing to his name, for he is gracious" (135:3). In this second kind of praise, the author gives praise without regard for the things God gives to him.

The difference between these two kinds of praise is not that the first is based on selfish considerations whereas the second is not. For there is nothing selfish about receiving forgiveness and sustenance and health from God. We would say that the Psalmist was being selfish if he praised God for making him a highly esteemed Temple worshiper or for adding to his already abundant herd of sheep. If the Psalmist intended only to obtain self-aggrandizing benefits from God, he would be using God for his selfish aims. In such a case we would be inclined to say that what the Psalmist is calling praise is nothing more than payment intended to keep benefits coming.

The difference between the two kinds of praise is that the first is linked to receiving something from God whereas the second is not linked to receiving anything from God. In the first kind, we praise God for the good things he has done for us. In the second, we praise God solely for the excellence of his character — his boundless love and pure goodness. This kind of praise is engaged in for its own sake, simply because it is fitting. "How good it is to sing praises to our God; for he is gracious, and a song of praise is fitting," exclaims the Psalmist (147:1). Thus, whereas the first kind of praise derives from self-directed (though not selfish) motives, the second derives from other-directed or self-forgetful motives.

This difference has been noticed by a variety of writers, both Christian and non-Christian. In discussing what counts as genuine love for God, Jonathan Edwards writes that those who love God are "inexpressibly pleased and delighted with the . . . things of God." This love is of two kinds, one of which comes from the gratefulness of those who love God, and the other of which comes from their perception "of the beautiful and delightful nature of divine things." Edwards calls the first kind "self-love," but in so doing he does not intend to demean it. "Self-love is not excluded from a gracious gratitude; the saints love God for his kindness to them, 'I love the Lord, because he hath heard the voice of my supplication' (Ps. 116:1). But something else is included; and another love prepares the way, and lays the foundation, for these grateful affections." This something else is delight in God's perfection; those who have this delight "rejoice in God as glorious and excellent in himself."[2]

Edwards distinguishes both of these kinds of love from the pseudo-love of self-interest. Those who have this pseudo-love "first rejoice, and are elevated with it, that they are made so much of by God; and then on that ground, he seems in a sort, lovely to them." These individuals love God only for the ego-expanding advantages they get from God. Christ's love "exalts" these individuals, "vastly distinguishing some from others," so that "their joy is really a joy in themselves, and not in God." They talk about their own experience of God instead of God himself. The person whose love is not based on self-interest, however, is "too much captivated and engaged by what he views without himself, to stand at that time to view himself, and his own attainments."[3]

2. Edwards, *Treatise on Religious Affections* (New Haven: Yale University Press, 1959), pp. 248, 250.
3. Ibid., pp. 250, 251, 252.

Some writers have characterized the attitude in other-directed praise as "disinterestedness." By this they mean that when we offer disinterested praise, it contains no interest in any selfish gain or self-regarding benefit. Our interest is focused entirely on the object of our attention. "The admiration, joy, or love turns wholly upon what is exterior and foreign to ourselves."[4] We abandon ourselves to the object and detach ourselves from the desire to possess it or use it for any end other than attending to it, no matter how good the end is.[5] Arthur Schopenhauer, a nineteenth-century German philosopher, observed this kind of abandonment and detachment in aesthetic contemplation. In this state we focus on things "without interest," he wrote; we become "lost in the object" and achieve a state of "forgetting" ourselves. He also noted that this state is as rare as it is elevated. "Who has the strength to remain in it for long?" he asked.[6]

In *God, Guilt, and Death*, Merold Westphal undertakes an in-depth treatment of the difference between a self-regarding attitude toward God and a disinterested one. He designates the latter attitude "useless self-transcendence." When we have this attitude, we do not use God to satisfy our needs, but instead open ourselves to the divine presence. When we do this, it is useless not because it is of no value but because we have no goal beyond being in God's presence. What we do is a "terminal" activity with no further end. In addition, we transcend ourselves by letting go of our infatuation with the self, and by giving the self to God. This letting go and giving is something beyond the self. We lose ourselves in something outside us.[7]

Westphal notes that useless self-transcendence is exhibited in

---

4. Anthony, Earl of Shaftesbury, quoted by Jerome Stolnitz in "On the Origins of 'Aesthetic Disinterestedness,'" *The Journal of Aesthetics and Art Criticism* 20 (1961): 134.

5. Ibid., pp. 136, 137.

6. Schopenhauer, *The World as Will and Representation*, vol. 1, trans. E. F. J. Payne (New York: Dover Publications, 1989), pp. 196-99.

7. Westphal, *God, Guilt, and Death: An Existential Phenomenology of Religion* (Bloomington: Indiana University Press, 1984), Chapter 7, "Religion as Means and as End," and Chapter 8, "Prayer and Sacrifice as Useless Self-Transcendence," pp. 122-59. See especially pp. 133, 138-39, 145.

various Christian practices. Church worship is in part a self-abandoning celebration of the presence of God. Participating in communion, the eucharist, or the mass is in part a self-displacing sacrifice. Praise involves self-surrender, and in prayer "adoration more and more takes charge." To be sure, these activities are mixed with a desire to receive benefits, Westphal observes. In participating in communion we are given assurance of divine forgiveness, and in offering prayer we ask for inner peace. The presence of these self-regarding motives does not mean, however, that useless self-transcendence is absent or somehow undermined. Both are, or can be, present in a single activity. "Sacrifice is as much a giving as a receiving."[8]

These writers have accurately described the Psalmist's self-forgetful praise. Although the Psalmist does not say so, this praise is profoundly fulfilling, not as the satisfaction of a self-regarding desire, but as the completion of our deep longing to give ourselves to something divine. Perhaps a significant share of life's restless striving is motivated by this often unrecognized longing.

Some of these same things are also true of being aware of moral beauty in people. Being aware of moral beauty requires the same displacement of the self that other-directed praise of God requires. It is a terminal activity in that it aims at no end beyond itself and it fulfills a deep yearning to give ourselves away.

Seeing Moral Beauty in Others

On the evening just prior to a particularly vicious battle in the Napoleonic wars of 1808, a group of Russian soldiers sat around a fire, reminiscing. One of the soldiers, who was torn to pieces the next day by a French cannonball, was telling tales of "moral beauty."

In this scene, depicted by Leo Tolstoy in *War and Peace,* the reader cannot help noticing the contrast between the war's fierceness and the soldiers' unhurried respite from it. The same is true of the contrast between the ordinariness of the reminiscing and the captivating nature of the stories.

8. Ibid., pp. 141-43, 146-48, 157.

Tolstoy does not tell us what he conceives moral beauty to be. He simply slips the phrase into his narrative without so much as a pause. Yet it is worth a million pauses.

In this section I shall describe what it is to see moral beauty in people and note several obstacles to doing so. I shall also describe what perceiving moral beauty does to us and to those in whom we observe it. I will begin with a few examples.

In his moving allegory entitled *The Story of the Other Wise Man,* Henry van Dyke describes the self-sacrifice of the Magian who was prevented from accompanying the three wise men on their journey to Bethlehem. He was to have met them at an appointed hour, but he was detained by the plaintive cry of a dying man whom he stopped to nurse back to life. Although he desperately wanted to go to Bethlehem, and although he knew the three would leave without him if he did not hurry, he spent a considerable amount of time restoring the health of the dying man.

There are numerous less dramatic instances that we may encounter in routine circumstances. Imagine that two friends are talking together over lunch. Their conversation ranges over a number of everyday concerns. At one point one of them expresses insecurity, both by her tone of voice and by what she says. The other seizes the opportunity to give her assurance. "You're special, Ann, and you've meant a lot to me."

Imagine next that half a dozen people have given up one of their Saturdays to help fix up an inner-city mission. During a break, as they sit talking about city life, one of them remarks quietly, "It is the love of Christ in my heart that brings me here."

Imagine, finally, that two friends are talking to each other about their inner lives. One of them explains to the other that the reason she has remained aloof from men for so long and has not been able to trust them is that she was never sure that her father cared about her as a child. For ten years she told herself that it didn't matter anyway, but now she has discovered that it does matter, and she resents her father for not loving her. "But," she adds, "perhaps he wasn't able to give me what I needed." Her friend asks, "Does that amount to a kind of forgiveness of your father?" "Yes, I guess it does," she replies.

To see the moral beauty in each of these situations is to delight in the assurance given, the love expressed, and the forgiveness realized. It is to be struck by these, to remember them, and to savor them. What happens is the same thing that happens when we observe physical beauty. A distinctive feature of an otherwise ordinary circumstance stands out in our consciousness, and we take keen enjoyment in being aware of it.

Seeing this distinctive feature requires sensitivity. Two people may look at the still, precise reflection of a tree in a perfectly calm pond, but only one may see the beauty in it. So, too, the beauty in each of the preceding examples may escape our notice unless we prize highly the distinctiveness in them.

Friedrich Nietzsche, a nineteenth-century philosopher, was responsive to a deeper dimension of life. Unfortunately, what he saw was not beauty but ugliness. In the section of his autobiography entitled "Why I Am So Wise," he tells us that his "instinct for cleanliness is characterized by a perfectly uncanny sensitivity so that the inmost parts of every soul are perceived by me — *smelled*." This sensitivity, he explains, "furnishes me with psychological antennae with which I feel every secret: the abundant *hidden* dirt at the bottom of many a character."9

Although we may react to this passage with disgust, we find in it two images that illumine the sensitivity required for seeing moral beauty. Nietzsche tells us that his perception of the inner lives of people is instinctive. He has a natural aptitude for observing what lies behind a person's exterior. Nietzsche also tells us that his ability to sense what goes on inside others is like having antennae. Antennae pick up signals that are not observable by ordinary means. Using these antennae, Nietzsche is able to perceive what to other people is hidden.

When we are sensitive to moral beauty in people, we instinctively notice the moral and spiritual dimension of their lives. Our spiritual antennae pick up what otherwise we would not give a second thought. Assurance, love, and forgiveness attract our attention.

9. Nietzsche, *Ecce Homo*, Section 8, in *"On the Genealogy of Morals" and "Ecce Homo,"* trans. Walter Kaufmann (New York: Vintage Books, 1967), p. 233.

We are not, however, always drawn to the good that we see. In fact, our instincts sometimes are to look for the bad, and we often notice that more easily than the good.

There are several reasons why moral beauty does not strike us as vigorously as it could. First, one of our basic impulses is to be more interested in ourselves than in others. Seeing moral beauty requires just the reverse. And this demands a selflessness that we rarely have — indeed, that we often would rather not have.

Moreover, our routine cares sap the effort, reduce the hunger for righteousness and the thirst for goodness, required to perceive moral beauty. We seldom have much energy beyond what we need to get through each day's activities. We usually have just enough to perform our duties and give ourselves a few compensating pleasures. This inertia afflicts us in varying degrees. Sometimes it is all we can do simply to stay alive; we have little energy left over for extras. When we are in such a state, moral beauty is not likely to matter much to us.

Finally, we are prone to be envious of the good qualities in others. Envy is not simply a desire to possess the qualities or achievements of other people. It is also a painful and resentful awareness of these qualities. The awareness is painful because we see others' qualities and successes as diminishing our own worth. So instead of valuing those qualities and achievements, we tend to dismiss them from consciousness or deny their beauty.

The remedy for envy is a sense of inner security. This sense comes to us when we accept the fact that our worth rests not on our qualities and achievements but on God's acceptance of us. Accepting this fact frees us from the impulse to see other people's qualities and achievements as detracting from our worth. We can look at these and appreciate them, enjoy them, even delight in them, without being bombarded with doubts about ourselves or critical thoughts about others.

To be sensitive to moral beauty, then, requires an inner transformation: release from preoccupation with ourselves, spiritual energy, and a continuing consciousness of God's acceptance of us. Because we wrestle with these our whole lives, being sensitive to beauty in others is a never-ending struggle. But when we begin to be transformed in these ways, not only are we able to see beauty, but we actively look for it. We develop a fascination with knowing others — their hopes, fears, and struggles, their loving, giving, and selflessness. We become alert to particular instances of these, both in people we read about and in people we know, whom we see every day.

The perception of moral beauty is not an optional feature of our new lives in Christ, for it springs from the basic changes that occur when Christ remakes us. He gives us a thirst for goodness and a hunger for righteousness. He fills us with a sense of gratitude for grace received, which incites us to behold with awe the same gift in others.

Although there is no formula for finding moral beauty, there are definite steps we can take in seeking it. We can set aside our own cares and worries for a time and focus our attention on others. We can turn off our televisions and visit our friends. We can ask about their activities, thoughts, and feelings, and listen actively to what they tell us. What we will find is that the search for moral beauty is a creative adventure filled with pleasant surprises.

We may not find numerous instances of moral beauty, but those we discover will be meaningful and will impress themselves deeply into our memory. We will listen to the laugh of a person who has been seriously depressed, observe others showing sacrificial love for society's rejects, and see the smile on the once-tear-stained face of a person who has suffered a devastating loss. We will learn of the struggle of someone who is grappling with a lifelong difficulty, see the joy in a person who has just discovered God's forgiving love, and notice warmth in people whom we had hitherto thought of as distant. We will hear the story of someone who has rebounded from bouts of despair, and come to know the pilgrimage of a person who has given up impediments to spiritual growth.

On occasion we will come across what Dostoyevsky calls a "truly beautiful soul." Dostoyevsky wrote his magnificent novel entitled *The Idiot* in order to depict just such a person. Innocence is a prominent characteristic of Dostoyevsky's creation, not the unknowing innocence of childhood but purity of heart despite acquaintance with evil. Willingness to forgive, unadulterated simplicity, gentleness, and instinctive compassion are further features of this character.

A truly beautiful soul has other qualities as well. It loves genuinely and openly, with a deep-felt interest in the concerns of others. It refuses to hold the failings of others against them. It is patient in spite of interruptions and kind in spite of offense. Its love for life is evident and its giving is extravagant. It is sensitive to the feelings of others, and it constantly gives encouragement. It has, in M. Scott Peck's words, a "gracefulness of existence."[10]

What effects does being aware of moral beauty have? From one perspective this is the wrong question to ask, since being aware of moral beauty is worthwhile apart from its effects. Simply becoming aware of instances of love, forgiveness, joy, and gentleness enriches our lives. It is one of the things that makes life worth living, and possessing such awareness is desirable for its own sake.

From another perspective, however, this question is important, because being aware of moral beauty has significant effects both on ourselves and on others. When we observe moral beauty, we take it into ourselves. It becomes part of our lives, and if we have not been in the habit of noticing it, we can feel the change that takes place in us when we do begin noticing it.

The principle that operates here is the same as that which operates when we observe evil. If we were to look for instances of evil in people whom we know and let these instances soak into our consciousness, we would find ourselves being changed. Our outlook on life would become cynical, we would develop an antagonistic attitude toward others, possibly becoming bitter and sour, and the memories of these instances would linger on, perhaps even haunt us.

It is the same with moral beauty. When we absorb it, we cannot help but be affected. Our disposition becomes brighter, we give ourselves to others ungrudgingly, and we treasure memories of distinctive occasions on which we see and experience moral beauty. The gloom we feel when we are involved with other people's troubles loses its oppressiveness. We see that this is God's world after all.

We find too that some of our deepest yearnings are fulfilled.

10. Peck, *People of the Lie: The Hope for Healing Human Evil* (New York: Simon & Schuster, 1983), p. 125.

We crave moments in which we lose ourselves. This happens when we admiringly behold the beauty in someone in a way that is akin to self-forgetful praise of God. We long to gaze at untarnished goodness, and this occurs to a degree when we glimpse it in our friends. These yearnings are, to be sure, obscured and thwarted by self-centeredness, but they are in us, and their fulfillment produces a deep sense of life's meaningfulness, quieting our restless hearts and subduing our ceaseless strivings.

Moreover, we treat people differently when we see beauty in them. Because we have high regard for them, we treat them with respect and care, even with some tenderness. It would be entirely different if, like Nietzsche, we were to see dirt and ugliness. Then we would treat people with scorn and contempt, with little sensitivity to their feelings or rights.

Being aware of moral beauty also has a direct effect on the people themselves. They often sense what we see in them. They notice the expressions on our faces and pick up signals from our behavior toward them. Our delight clearly shows in our eyes, in much the same way that a certain radiancy emanates from a person who is falling in love. This delight is a clear message to them that we have seen something that we value highly.

Nietzsche knew about this phenomenon. Of those in whom he detected "hidden dirt," he wrote, "Such characters who offend my sense of cleanliness also sense from their side the reserve of my disgust."[11] St. Francis of Assisi may also have known about this phenomenon. It is said that one of the reasons he had such extraordinary magnetism was that those who gazed into his eyes saw displayed there an unfeigned interest in their individual lives.[12]

At times our delight will overflow, and we will tell people what

11. Nietzsche, *Ecce Homo*, p. 233.

12. "What gave him extraordinary personal power was this; that . . . there was never a man who looked into those brown burning eyes without being certain that Francis Bernardone was really interested in *him*, in his own inner individual life from the cradle to the grave; that he himself was being valued and taken seriously" (G. K. Chesterton, quoted by Donald P. McNeill, Douglas A. Morrison, and Henri J. M. Nouwen in *Compassion: A Reflection on the Christian Life* [Garden City, N.Y.: Doubleday–Image Books, 1983], p. 68).

we see. We might say, "What I like about you is . . ." or "I love the way you . . ." or "It was nice of you to . . ."

The fascinating thing about people knowing what we see in them is that they are likely to act as we see them. If we see dirt, they will probably act dirty. If we see purity, they will have a tendency to act with purity. A piano player who is told "You play well" will practice harder. So, too, a Christian who is told "You really care about people" will care even more.

When once we have made awareness of moral beauty our habit, we will discover that on occasion we will have to look past the sins and shortcomings of those in whom we would see beauty. Here, perhaps, is the greatest obstacle to the practice. It will seem to us nearly impossible to think of someone as doing something beautiful when we know how that person has fallen. This is especially true if the person has hurt us in some way — with an unkind word, for example. In such cases, looking for beauty becomes a form of love, not an easy love that dissipates with affront but a hard love that hangs on in spite of offense.

In *War and Peace,* Princess Marya, just after declining a marriage proposal, thinks to herself, "My vocation is a different one. My vocation is to be happy in the happiness of others."[13] It is not just any happiness she exults in; it is, she adds, "the happiness of love and self-sacrifice." Although she is mistaken about the incompatibility of marriage and being happy in the happiness of others, Princess Marya chose exactly the right word to describe awareness of moral beauty. It is a vocation, inextricably intertwined with every part of our lives.

The Swollen Eye

Some years ago I visited a church service held by the Jesus People (a Christian commune) on the north side of Chicago. At that time about 10 percent of those who attended their Sunday morning

---

13. Tolstoy, *War and Peace,* trans. Constance Garnett (New York: Modern Library, n.d.), p. 210.

services were street people — mostly alcoholic, homeless men. They usually sat by themselves on a row of chairs in the back of the large, basement-like room where gatherings and common meals were held.

On the Sunday I visited, a street person sat one row in front of me and three chairs to my left. Like most of the street people there, he wore ill-fitting, dirty clothes. Unlike the others, he was noticeably hurt: his right eye was completely swollen shut. The areas just above and below his eye had become so puffy that they covered his eye entirely. A bloody gash above his right eyebrow explained the presence of this hideous sight.

I didn't listen very well to the sermon that morning because I kept stealing glances at the unshaven face with the unseeing eye. In addition to pity, I felt a bit of revulsion. How could anyone be attracted to this unkempt man, or think there was anything beautiful about him?

The sermon finally ended, and we sang a song, prayed, and stood to leave. The street person with one good eye turned and walked straight toward me. He extended his hand, smiled broadly, and greeted me with a gravelly but genuine "Hello. How are you?" I was too astonished to respond with anything more than a weak handshake and a dull smile. But his face — dirty, unshaved, and battered as it was — had a real smile on it.

Chapter 9

Conclusion: Singleness and the Pursuit of the Eternal

I wish to make people aware, so that they do not squander and dissipate their lives.

Kierkegaard, Journals

It is time to reflect on the themes we have looked at. What do they say about human nature? Is there a way to alleviate the sense of tragedy that arises when we think about dividedness? Can we overcome doubt about whether we can escape dividedness? I shall begin with the implications of what I have said for human nature.

On Human Nature

One cannot look at ambivalence and illusion for long without coming to the conclusion that there is "a rupture in the recesses of human nature."[1] We are split beings at a level not easily accessible to everyday observation. This split exhibits itself in our attraction both to self-directed motives and to self-forgetful praise of God. It accounts

1. G. van der Leeuw, *Religion in Essence and Manifestation: A Study in Phenomenology* (London: George Allen & Unwin, 1938), p. 466.

both for the massive amount of pretending we engage in and for our intense aversion to pretending. It explains why we desperately want to hide our ulterior motives from ourselves and also why we just as strongly want to unmask them. It even shows itself in our ambivalent attitude toward the split itself. We want both to acknowledge dividedness and to evade acknowledging it, both to escape it and to retain it. Living with dividedness is somehow both torturous and gratifying.

I want now to relate this feature of human nature to three theological concepts — prefall innocence, the fall into sin, and the restoration that occurs after death. The account of human nature that together these three concepts present is one in which our current state is an interlude. Human beings once were without the pain and turmoil that sin brings, and those who are recipients of God's saving grace will be without them again. In between, we experience agonies of various sorts, many of our own making. If we render this account in terms of singleness and doubleness, we get the following characterization.

During the time of prefall innocence, human beings loved without expecting any reward for doing so. They gave simply for the sake of giving and did things without noticing how these things compared with what other people did. They did not retreat into imagination to escape a feeling of unworth or keep busy to avoid the pain of self-revealing introspection. They put on none of the pretensions we now put on. They were, in short, without any of the ambivalence and illusion that we currently possess.

After our lifelong struggle with dividedness, we will be restored to something like prefall innocence. We will not have the same unknowingness that people had then, for we will remember the times we wanted others to notice our virtues and the occasions we helped others so we could think of ourselves as heroes. We will recall that for years we pretended to be Christian. But these memories will be bathed in God's healing love, which we will receive without the resistance we now have. It may be painful to receive his love at that time, for it will burn away our beloved self-admiration and pretension, but we will nevertheless receive it without doing so for ulterior motives.

In the interlude between these two periods, we live with both a love and a hate of our "dreads" — self-admiration, self-justification, and comparisons.[2] This division comes from two sources: the fall, which introduced desires unknown in the prefall period, and the continuation, to a degree, of the desires people possessed before the fall. If there were not in our current state vestiges of that prefall innocence, we would not experience dividedness at all. We would experience an unadulterated love of self-admiration and self-justification. But we hate them as well as love them. So we must have retained the desires we once had. Though the fall has blunted these desires, it has not obliterated them.

This characterization of the three states is not a reinterpretation of the traditional doctrines. It is a way of explaining how they are evidenced in our inner life. Of course, no one has ever claimed that the cosmic drama of which we are a part cannot be conceived in terms of the inner life. But because we have an aversion to knowing what goes on inside us, we tend to think of the three states principally in terms of public actions. Part of the point, then, of exploring dividedness is to remind ourselves that these major motifs in Christianity — creation, fall, and redemption — may also be thought of in terms of desires.

By linking dividedness to these three states, we also put our current condition into long-range perspective. Though the rupture in our nature seems to be a natural part of us because we live with it every day, it is really an aberration. From the perspective of eternity, our true nature consists of desires that are unmixed with impulses of self-justification and self-admiration. These prefall desires are now mostly suppressed and hidden, but there was a time when they were not, and there will be a time when they will not be concealed. Immersed as we are in dividedness, we are rarely conscious of this long-range perspective. Even so, there are times when we recognize, perhaps faintly, that our moments of cosmic wistfulness are longings to return to a state of unmixed desires and that our restless sighings are yearnings for restoration.

---

2. Van der Leeuw writes, "We all realize, in truth, that we not only hate our dreads, but also, in secret, love them" (ibid., p. 466).

The Tragic Sense of Life

There is another kind of dividedness which, unlike the forms I have described, is desirable to have. This kind arises when we reflect on the significance of our ambivalence. It is the recognition that because of our ambivalence, life is tragic, and that our moments of undivided love are beautiful.

The kind of tragedy with which we are most familiar is the kind in which overt events and actions do not fit our conception of what is good or desirable. People are killed when they are much too young to die; children are hit, raped, or abandoned by their parents. An accident blinds someone, or a person's spouse becomes alcoholic and violent.

The tragedy that exists because of ambivalence is the kind in which inner states do not fit our conception of what is good or desirable. From the perspective of what life could be like, it is a tragedy that we have secrets we are afraid to tell ourselves, that we pretend to ourselves to be what we are not, and that we both do and do not want God's healing love. It is tragic that we quietly gloat over the self-importance we get from loving the unloved and that we secretly revel in the admiration we receive for acting compassionately. It is also tragic that we both enjoy and feel ashamed of our secret gloating and reveling.

The tragedy of human dividedness is aptly described by Arthur Schopenhauer in his characterization of tragedy as an art form. "The purpose [of tragedy]," he writes, ". . . is the description of the terrible side of life." Schopenhauer specifies what he believes the terrible side of life to be: "It is the antagonism of the will with itself which is here most completely unfolded . . . , and which comes into fearful prominence."[3] When we feel the discrepancy between the antagonism of the will with itself and our vision of a single-minded pursuit of eternity, we sense that life is tragic. And when we feel this discrepancy in ourselves, we sense that our own lives are tragedies. Kierkegaard must have felt this sense of tragedy keenly, not only about

3. Schopenhauer, *The World as Will and Representation*, vol. 1, trans. E. F. J. Payne (New York: Dover Publications, 1969), pp. 252, 253.

humankind but about himself. His books are filled with traces of a desperate soul searching for release from acute inner conflict. One commentator observes, "His deepest sorrow was that he failed to achieve that degree of inner unity which would have allowed him, with a new spontaneity . . . , in one single ardent, confident leap, to become the knight of faith."[4]

From one perspective, having a sense of tragedy is itself tragic, for we can conceive of life without either tragedy or dividedness. From another perspective, it is a fortunate affliction to possess, for it is a call from eternity. With it we feel deeply the loss of singleness, and we ache for the end of dividedness. The sense of tragedy heightens our longing for unmixed desires and intensifies our homesickness for a state without internal clashes. "It is the sickness which is the greatest misfortune not to have,"[5] for to be without it is to be indifferent to dividedness.

The tragic sense of life, however, can also be the most dangerous sickness of all.[6] Since all is spoiled by dividedness, we may feel that nothing about life is worthwhile — and there is nothing more crushing than a sense that our whole life is a loss. If the tragic sense of life were our only perspective, and if we did not perceive it as a call from eternity, we would become victims of incapacitating sadness.

One way, perhaps the only way, of avoiding this sadness without giving up the sense of life as tragic is to balance this sense with an awareness of life's beauty. One side of ambivalent dyads, after all, is good. That the dyad itself is tragic does not make the good in it tragic. It is possible to hold in tension both the sense of tragedy and the awareness of beauty. If we conceive of our receiving and giving of grace as things of beauty (without doing so in a self-admiring way), we will temper the disabling sadness caused by the consciousness of tragedy.

4. Regis Jolivet, *Introduction to Kierkegaard,* trans. W. H. Barber (New York: E. P. Dutton, 1952), p. 59.

5. Liselotte Richter, "Kierkegaard's Position in His Religio-Sociological Situation," in *A Kierkegaard Critique,* ed. Howard A. Johnson and Niels Thulstrup (New York: Harper, 1962), p. 67. Richter makes this claim about Kierkegaardian despair.

6. "Despair . . . is the most dangerous disease of all if one does not want to be cured of it" (ibid., p. 68).

Doubt and Certainty

It is also possible to hold in tension both doubt and certainty. It is in fact necessary to do so if we are to avoid the despair that doubt brings and the complacency that certainty causes.

Perhaps the first, and most lasting, reaction to exploring motives that undermine singleness of heart is doubt about whether we can recognize illusory experiences of grace. The motives are embedded so deeply and extend so widely that we cannot help but wonder despairingly whether we can ever become aware of them. There is, we perceive, a great deal at stake in this matter. One of the most basic human needs is the need to know what our cosmic status is. Christianity claims that we can know this only if we can know what our relation is to the One upon whom that status depends. So if we are unable to discover when the undermining motives are causing illusion in us, we cannot be sure what position we are in. We might really be lost even though we think we are saved. Our restless quest for certainty would be frustrated, and we would be unable to get one of the things we most want in life.

Moreover, if we cannot know what our cosmic position is, the Bible would be mocking us in presenting a picture of what that position should be. From the beginning chapters of Genesis to the last chapters of Revelation, the Bible tells us how God wants us to be. God wants us to center our affection on him rather than on money, clothes, sex, power, and ego-expanding praise; he wants us to recognize that we have done the reverse, to accept his love for us anyway, and to turn our affection back to him. If we cannot know that we have accepted his love and have turned our affection to him, God would be making sport of us by telling us to do something we cannot know we are doing. So if we take the Bible seriously, we must believe that we can know we are in the position the Bible says we should be in.

This is something we can know, as was demonstrated in Chapter Six. We can use the three tests described there to assess our experiences of grace. We can compare them with what we know experiences of grace are not, we can compare them with what we know they are, and we can observe what effects they have.

It is dangerous, however, to believe that we have this knowledge without also retaining doubt. In the first place, we may be mistaken in thinking that we have the knowledge, for we may not have detected all the motives that can bring about an illusory experience of grace. An additional, undetected motive may be causing us to think that we are open to grace even though we are not. Both comparison and selfadmiration may be operative, and though ascertaining one makes it likely that we will ascertain the other, this will not automatically happen.

Moreover, after we uncover one illusory experience, a new one might emerge. We may at first discover that what we took to be an encounter with grace was nothing more than an intense episode of self-admiration. But after unearthing this self-admiration, we might later discover that another form of self-justification has crept in. Or we might find that fresh outbreaks of the original self-admiration have occurred in subtler and more underhanded ways. These subsequent occurrences would not undercut the validity of a prior experience of grace. They would, however, undermine our ability to continue to have that experience. If we do not maintain continuing doubt about our motives, we are likely never to notice the creeping in of new motives or the fresh outbreaks of old ones. We almost certainly will become victims of the tenacious impulse to point at Pharisees.

This continuing doubt is not the "We cannot know" of skepticism, for skepticism is incompatible with the knowledge we obtain from using the three tests. The doubt with which we need to temper certainty is a searching doubt. It consists of a perpetual attitude of self-scrutiny, of not being content with the way we are, of poking around behind appearances, and of interrogating ourselves. It is the propensity to pursue relentlessly. Maintaining it indicates that we sense eternity's call.

To be sure, this doubt can cripple. It can cause us to turn inward too much and make us think that we will never know what our status with God is. It can undermine the delight and adventure that being open to grace brings. It can produce hopelessness both about human nature and about our own ability to elude ambivalence and illusion.

In spite of these risks, doubt is necessary, for without it we are not likely to move toward singleness of heart. Though it may seem paradoxical, a childlike faith requires the very thing which, if indulged in, would undermine it.

Epilogue

I began this book by remarking that the Christian heart is a strange paradox. Now we see that it is no longer so strange. We know why we like being ambivalent and why we persist in illusion. We have unmasked the motives that make us spiritual schizophrenics. It is no wonder, we say with a sad shake of our heads, that we live outside ourselves.

Still, the strangeness persists. There is intrigue in a rejuvenated existence that will not give up its illusions, uncomprehending wonder about a being that anxiously flees the love it so delights in, knowing that it flees but convincing itself that it does not. Who can grope to the bottom of such a thing?

Perhaps we must leave matters this way: the Christian heart is both tragic and beautiful, both torn and mended, a truth we need to embrace with both despair and confidence. Though it casts out the grace it longs for, it also lets itself be healed by this grace. If we recognize these oppositions, we will have made progress in our journey toward restoration.